Edward Churton

Poetical Remains

Edward Churton

Poetical Remains

ISBN/EAN: 9783337778002

Printed in Europe, USA, Canada, Australia, Japan

Cover: Foto ©Thomas Meinert / pixelio.de

More available books at **www.hansebooks.com**

POETICAL REMAINS

OF

EDWARD CHURTON, M.A.

RECTOR OF CRAYKE AND ARCHDEACON OF CLEVELAND

LONDON
JOHN MURRAY, ALBEMARLE STREET
1876

PREFACE.

The history of this little volume is simply as follows :—

In days of severe public anxiety, when each new peril and distress of the Church was felt to their very heart's core by her faithful and ardent sons, and also in seasons of physical depression arising in the course of many years, my father ever found in Poetry his refreshment and restorative. Often, after long hours at his desk, he used to take a short respite in his garden, with a Spanish poem in his pocket for reference if necessary, and, while busily raking or weeding his lawn, or in winter pacing up and down a favourite terrace-walk, would set himself to "turn" or "mend" a Sonnet. Then he would come in, with eyes brightened and brow cleared, to give us the result of his "play-time." To him the repose of inaction was an impossibility; his only rest in waking hours was in change of exercise; and in this way his strenuous spirit did most thoroughly "relish versing" even to old age. This then is the true account of most of the following translations: they were the play of his most laborious years. For his children's holiday amusement he translated three very interesting Spanish plays, besides a large number of ballads, spirited or grotesque, which were thrown off with great rapidity, and appear hardly to have been looked at again. As these translations accumulated, he sometimes talked of making a selection from them for publication, thinking the ballad-lore of other lands full of interest, and especially delighting himself in the treasures of old Spanish poetry, abounding as it does in the generous fire and quaint humour which always had peculiar charms for him. The selection was never made by himself, and the work has now been undertaken in obedience to his wishes, but with much diffidence, without sufficient knowledge of the original sources to guide to a due estimate of the merit of the translation, and with the consciousness that none of these poems had received the last touches of their Author. It is hoped, however, that if some of these translations are found to lack the accurate finish which characterises the Author's versions of *Gongora*, the sparkles of native fun and fire, which in their own tongue first attracted *him*, may, even in their English dress, sufficiently plead for their acceptance.

Of the Original Poems previously published by himself little need now be said, except in acknowledgment of the kind permission of Mr. Masters and the Rev. Orby Shipley to reprint those which formerly appeared under their auspices.

But of those now first published, it is right to own that they were never intended for the public. Some of these, which, though few in number, form no unimportant part of the whole collection, were most truly, in accordance with Wordsworth's definition of poetry, "the spontaneous overflow of powerful feelings"; the strong deep fount within swelling up and finding its only vent in verse; and these, apart from their intrinsic merit, will have a special interest for those who loved him, as bearing, in some sense more truly than anything he ever wrote for publication, the impress of his inner self.

It was thought that the portraiture would be incomplete without one or two specimens, out of very many, of the playful sallies which were wont to celebrate holiday adventures or merry misadventures for the amusement of his children; but it has proved almost impossible to give a fair sample of this sort, the sportive allusions being for the most part hardly intelligible to any but the initiated.

It will be seen from some of the following poems that his love for the great poets of his youth became only stronger and more appreciative in his age. Wordsworth, Southey, and Walter Scott, he continued to delight in quite to the end. Dante he had studied in early manhood, a pursuit shared with a beloved sister;* and his memory of many passages in the *Divina Commedia* remained undimmed even in his last illness. Tasso was a great favourite; and, not unworthy to be named with Tasso, Fairfax, his unrivalled translator. And then, the great masters of English song, "the sage and serious poet Spenser" especially, were from youth to age beloved and familiar friends. And so, through a life of unremitting labour, quiet and peaceful in outward surroundings, but in reality a life of diligent work and earnest conflict, Poetry was to him the "finer breath of being," † a friend whose voice—to apply Thomas Whytehead's beautiful words—was like

"A sound of church-bells on a working day."

S. M. I.

CRAYKE, *July* 9, 1875.

---

* Anne, second daughter of Archdeacon Ralph Churton, who died at the age of nineteen. † Wordsworth.

CONTENTS.

	PAGE
SUNDAY MORNING, after travelling in a Mail all night; the light dawning over a meadow near King's Sutton	1
"IN MEMORIAM MEORUM"—	
II. A. P.	5
Fragment in a time of Sorrow, upon remembrance of a happy youthful Dream	6
William Ralph Churton	8
IN MEMORIAM W. R. C. BY F. C. M.	13
HIGH FORCE	21
A THOUGHT IN SUNSHINE	24
LAMMAS DAY	26
MY NEIGHBOUR'S LANDMARK	31
LAYS OF FAITH AND LOYALTY—	
1. The Little Martyr	39
2. Alaric the Goth	44
3. The Caliph and his Physician	54
4. Saint Edmund of East Anglia	60
5. A Story of Saint Olave	76
6. The Cid and Don Martin of Asturia	79
7. Saint Bernard's Younger Brother	87
8. Walter Espec	92
9. Margaret Bisset	102
10. The Boy of Navarre	110

CONTENTS.

LAYS OF FAITH AND LOYALTY—*Continued*—

	PAGE
11. The Battle of Varna	115
12. Lord Strafford	120
13. Sampson Horton	129
14. Elisabeth Stuart	134

TWO SONNETS, meditated in Grasmere Churchyard	141
SONNET. A Vision of the Hills	143
TWO SONNETS. Thoughts of Robert Southey	144
DEDICATORY SONNET prefixed to the Author's *Gongora*	146
SONNET. North-Country Rivers	147
IONA	148
KILLIECRANKIE	151
GLENCOE	153
A DIRGE AT CULLODEN	155
A. G. F. P.	159
NURSERY SONG. An Incident from the personal Memoirs of the River Wiske	160
"AD GULIELMUM MEUM"	163
A LAY TO THE LAST MINSTREL	167

TRANSLATIONS AND IMITATIONS.

FROM THE LATIN—

Vexilla Regis	185
Salvete, flores Martyrum	187

FROM THE ANGLO-SAXON—

The Resurrection, from Caedmon	188
From King Alfred	189
Fragment from the Metrical Calendar	191
Fragments from Aldhelm's Psalter	196
Metrical Paraphrase of the Apostles' Creed	199
Verses repeated by the Venerable Bede	204

CONTENTS.

FROM THE BRETON—
    The Death-Song of Gwenc'hlan 205
    Joan de Montfort 209

FROM THE CATALAN—
    Count Arnaldos 213
    The Soldan's Daughter 216
    The Stranger Child on Christmas Eve . . . 217
    The Prisoners of Lerida 219
    Don Juan and Don Raymond 222
    The Count of Eril 224
    Ballad of the War of the Succession . . . 226
    The Death of Bach de Roda 231
    The Doubtful Promise 234
    The Woman's-Tailor's Love 236
    "With Consent" 238
    Good-Night at Mallorca 240

FROM THE SPANISH—

  LUIS DE LEON—
    Hymn to Christ Crucified 242

  GONGORA—
    Carol on the Festival of the Presentation . . 248

  CALDERON—
    "Heav'n's Gifts of pardoning love" . . . 250
    The Power of Thought 251

  AN UNKNOWN AUTHOR—
    Dialogue of the Body and the Soul . . . 254

  VICENT GARCIA—
    To a very tall Lady, married to a little Man . . 259

  TOMAS DE YRIARTE—
    A Fable. The Ass's Provender 261
    A Fable. The Warrener and the Ferret . . 262
    Sonnet 264

CONTENTS.

SPANISH ROMANCES—
    The Captive 265
    Death of Durandarte 268
    Don Ramiro 272
AN ANDALUSIAN EPITAPH ON AN INFANT . . . 274

FROM MODERN SPANISH POETS—
    DON LLUIS ROCA. JOCHS FLORALS DE BARCELONA, 1860.
    The Dying Girl to her Mother 275

    DON ANTONIO DE TRUEBA: LIBRO DE LOS CANTARES.—LEIPZIG, 1860.
    Divided Hearts 278
    My Mother 284
    Love Immortal 289
    Song. The Herb-Maiden 295

SENOR BIENVENIDO Y CANO—
    Elegy on Arguelles, Calatrava, and Alvarez y Mendizabal, Ministers of Spain 296

FROM THE MODERN GREEK—
    "Why are the mountains overcast?" . . 299

SUNDAY MORNING.

AFTER TRAVELLING IN A MAIL ALL NIGHT; THE LIGHT DAWNING OVER A MEADOW NEAR KING'S SUTTON.

IT was the Sabbath morn; yet nought of life
Waked to its purple summons: couch'd in sleep
The careless herd still press'd the grassy dews,
Nor bird of dawning early matins sang.
Only the incense of the vale sent up
Mute Nature's adoration. Slowly then,
Scarce heard, the matin bell its soften'd chime
Pour'd on the gales of morning, and the sun
Gilded aloft the beauteous spire that rose
Far o'er the drooping mists of Cherwell's mead.

O where are now the worshippers whose prayer
Prevented the night-watches? Where the hymn
That in drear midnight rose? the lamps prepared
To hail the Bridegroom's Coming? Past the reign
Of solemn superstition; past is too
Devotion's deeper service. Who will wake
While others sleep, to plead and pray for them,
And wrestle for a blessing ere the dawn?

Or low in dust mourn darkling for the sins
Of Israel and his own, tuning his soul
To the sad prophet's harp, till from the East
It catch the tone of gladness, and mount up
To taste the fresh springs of immortal day?

July 25, 1824.

"In Memoriam Meorum."

"IT WAS THE MORNING HOUR."

"*I once was bless'd with such a matchless friend.*"

HENRY ANTONY PYE, born December 1799;
died September 14, 1823.

It was the morning hour, when dreams are true;
   And slumbers came, that, soothing long unrest,
   Still kept the theme of sorrow in my breast,
Yet cheer'd my spirit ere their visions flew:
I saw that long-loved form restored to view
   In more than mortal brightness: his pale eye
   Shone forth with more than earthly radiancy;
And from his cheek Consumption's withering hue
   Had fled; the bloom of ruddy health was there:
Methought he said, "it was no pain to die:"
   But, as I nearer press'd those sounds to hear,
He faded as a star in twilight dim;
Yet oh, the thought was sweet, that he was nigh,
That he was blest, and I once more with him.

                              1823.

FRAGMENT.

IN A TIME OF SORROW, UPON REMEMBRANCE OF A HAPPY YOUTHFUL DREAM.

Away, away,—it may not be
That heaven hath stored such joy for me:
E'en now this chequer'd scene of earth
Hath changed its fickle hue of mirth;
Pale slow Disease is brooding nigh,
And bids me turn my trembling eye
Where far above this vale of tears
Is built the Rock of endless years.

But oh! the bitter cup of pain!
The fiery throbs of mortal stain
That heave the wither'd heart within,
Ere to that blissful height it win!

The lustful sense, the roving glance,
The pang of pleasure's dreamy trance,
Of days mis-spent the fearful debt,
Canst thou recall, or Heaven forget?
How oft in Penitence' sad hour
Wild Fancy caught her faded flower,
And, reckless of remorse and pain,
Wove the strong cord of guilt again!

Father of Love! in good or ill
Thy Hand extends its mercy still.

By Thy inscrutable decree
Three youthful hearts that felt for me
Have one by one obtain'd that shore
Where sin and sorrow haunt no more.
I linger where their feet have stray'd;
Where oft the rapid hours delay'd,
While converse sweet in infant sense
Spoke more than manhood's eloquence:—
O Father, consecrate my grief,
And make me know that sole relief
Which from the Fount of Mercy streams
Beyond the bliss of morning dreams.

Feb. 9, 1828.

WILLIAM RALPH CHURTON.

NAT. SEPT. 8, 1801; OBIIT AUG. 29, 1828.

The bitter cup is past: that graceful form,
Bow'd down in death to feed the sullen worm,
Waits the glad voice, when heaven shall call its own
To change for virgin robes the charnel stone:
For oh! thy life was lovely, such as ne'er
The first-born's rapture taught a father's prayer;
And all the sainted wishes of thy breast
Met in one scope, to bless and to be blest!
  Yet knew we not our bliss: the pangs of sin
Chill'd our heart's blood, and turn'd all stone within;
Still hung we on those lips in mute despair,
Nor dared to trace Death's image sculptured there;
Till the sad father's heart with one brief groan
Mourn'd the pale corse that should have shrined his own,
And waked to living agonies the train
That ne'er on earth shall dream of joys again.*

---

  * "When we were all gathering round the bed of Death, unable to command our reason, or to speak except in groans and tears, weeping on each other's necks, my dear father alone seemed restored to new energy by the exceeding affliction. He summoned us to prayer,—'There is but One Resource in these afflictions;' and with unfaltering voice rendered thanks to God for the Christian life and death of the dear departed. O

One sleeps in dust before thee; he was gone
Ere yet to men his youth's fresh lustre shone:
His dark eye saw the tenth autumnal moon;
The grey oaks echo'd to his flute at noon;
But ere the grove its wintry honours shed
The sad nymphs mourn'd their young musician dead.*

A little longer thou :—the storied line
Of Greece and Albion's fairy lore were thine;
For thee the Muse unroll'd with placid eye
The spells that bathe young hearts in ecstasy:
Yet Truth thy first enchantment; taught to share
The peasant's humble meal, the peasant's prayer,
Hear the wise saws the village patriarch gave,
Mark his white locks, the blossoms of the grave,
Till, when with feeble eld his eye grew dim,
Or slow disease unnerved each vigorous limb,
Serene, with holy Paul, he sought release,
Drank of th' accustom'd fount, and died in peace.

And when the day of prayer returning stole
In solemn influence o'er thy gentle soul,

---

that I could remember the words! After this, he repeated once or twice, with a tone of deep feeling, the words of another bereaved parent: '*Ejus a me crematum est corpus, quod contra decuit ab illo meum!*' "—*E. C.'s Private Record.*

* John, fourth son of Ralph Churton and Mary his wife, born April 26, 1803.
"*obiit æt.* 11; *sepult. ap. Carth. Dom.*"
From R. C.'s Family Bible.

'Twas thine entranced to stray, at vernal prime;
In every pause that broke the distant chime,
From woodland knoll or fountain's side, to hear
Soft angels' music melting on thine ear;
And, ere the chilling night-dews bade retire,
Or yet the glow-worm lit her warning fire,
Lingering again to hail with hallow'd joy,—
Time, thy rude hand could ne'er that bliss destroy,—
Seen in the stillness of the Sabbath even,
The spire whose silent finger points to heaven!

   Then came the Parent's hour,—to hold to view
The maze of sorrows in a world he knew,
And point the truth divine, well understood
By thee, whose young heart felt a Saviour's blood.

   How could'st thou weep o'er saintly pilgrim's tale
Who trod the dews of Hermon's balmy vale,
Like gentle Heber, braved in forests rude
The glaring tiger's twilight solitude,
Or showed, in faith unmoved, the cross he bore
To men as wild on blue Ontario's shore!

   Those village scenes withdrew; the sacred seat
Of matron Science hail'd thy willing feet.
The turrets grey, for heav'nly musings made,—
The groves, where martyr spirits walk'd the shade,—
The cell, where oft, ere Plato's page had close,
O'er night's pale lamp the latticed morning rose,—
All these were thine, and gave, in glory won,
The palm that wreathes the Muses' darling son.

O fatal virtue!—spirit too divine
To dwell enthrall'd in this dim earthly shrine!
E'en now its narrow bounds thy genius scorn'd;
Those bright beams burnt the temple they adorn'd;
And through the beauteous ruin, pale and sere,
Shone like the lamp that gilds a sepulchre!
 Yet still thy vigorous step exulting led
Thy young compeers to Cumbrian mountain's head,
As firm as when, 'mid Alpine cliffs, it won
The glance that rapt dark Afric's warrior-son;
Or when thy manly arm was first to wake
The dawn's white surges on Benaco's lake,
What time, as startled by his ocean roar,*
The bright mist trembling fled the poplar shore.
 But now to holier cares thy hours were given,
By Thames' green marge, to visions full of heaven;
Or, midst the town's mad noise unchanged to pray,
And learn the Pastor's calm sequester'd way,
Beneath his fostering care,† who saw too soon
The fair flower fade before that sultry noon,
While yet its hues more lovely gave our eyes
The lustrous bloom of heaven's own paradise;
Till, all refined from grosser fumes, at last
Away the sweet ethereal spirit pass'd!

---

 * *Fremitu assurgens, Benace, marino.*—VIRGIL.

 † W. R. Churton was chaplain to the Bishop of London, W. Howley, afterwards Archbishop of Canterbury.

Forgive, just God, the griefs that would recall
The ransom'd virtue from Thy star-paved hall.
He was but shown on earth to teach us where
Our treasure is;—oh, let our hearts be there!
The tomb that closed on all that here could die;
The bursting throb's convulsive agony;
The heart's worn strings that seem'd to faint with pain;
The racking tempest of th' unquiet brain;
Oh! let them teach how far, far happier they,
Whose young life, borne on golden clouds away,
To meet Abijah's bliss, smiles on that shore
Where Faith, and Hope, and Love can mourn no
  more!

April 26, 1830.

It may be permitted to insert here,—in token of the enduring affection inspired by the beloved subject of the preceding lines, written by his brother in the freshness of bereavement,—the following stanzas, written thirty years later, by the truly fraternal friend of both, F. C. Massingberd, late Chancellor of Lincoln.

F. C. M. IN MEMORIAM W. R. C.

IMITATED FROM TENNYSON'S *In Memoriam.*

I.

It strikes upon a charmèd ear,
    That lay so mournfully sedate;—
    I am not used to dream of late;
I have not dream'd this many a year

Of him, who, in *my* prime of youth,
    Was call'd, for me too soon, away;
    But now I seem to know the day
Again, that brought me that stern truth.

He, too, was beautiful and good,
    All graces and all holiest lore
    Had oped for him their golden store
Whom Nature and the Muses woo'd.

Nor knew we, wearing near our heart
    How precious but how frail a treasure,
    Nor scann'd the days, nor found the measure
Of joy that should so soon depart.

II.

O well we lov'd those stately towers,
   Where Isis rolls his silent flood;
   Blithesome though various was the mood
With which we cull'd his classic flowers.

How joyful 'twas, at morning prime
   To meet upon our early way:
   To plan our labour for the day,
Then turn to catch the matin chime.

Sweet matin chime, from every tower
   Rung out to call his sons to prayer!
   And oh! more joyful yet, to share
Such greeting past, that solemn hour.

But most when he, the Man revered,
   Watching the "breeze" whose "rustling wing"
   Was "wakening every leaf to sing,"
The MINSTREL on our path appear'd.

III.

Nor less, in boyhood's happier hour
   By Avon's haunted bank we stood,
   Laved our young limbs in Swift's cold flood,
Or keenly proved mind's opening power.

O why so beautiful in youth?
   O why so good, so kind, so true?
   None fear'd, all loved thee, and the few,
Thy chosen friends, they loved in truth.

'Twas thine to weave in happiest verse
   Such words as purest thoughts inspire,
   Thoughts that might fit the holiest lyre,
Words such as angels might rehearse.

Oft, fired by thee, to joy and sport
   Thy comrades rush'd at evening "Play;"
   But oh! how memory rues the day
When play by fatal toil was bought!

IV.

And when those days of youth were o'er,
    And manhood's prime of hope was come,
    With thee I left my English home,
With thee I sought Italia's shore.

Still blithe of heart, and eager still
    For knowledge and for virtuous joy,
    Thine was the cup without alloy
Of those who love God's holiest will.

Haste, haste across fair Gallia's plain
    To track the Punic warrior's way,
    Where Isere's snow-born waters stray,
And Bernard's lesser height to gain.

"The Alps! the Alps!" with eager cheer
    Thine first to urge thy comrades on,
    The rushing crowd of thought in one
Is all combined:—"The Alps are here!"

V.

And where is *he*, unknown to fame
   As yet, though soon about to cast
   Undying memories o'er the past,
When all shall glow at ARNOLD'S name?

He, too, the leader of the train,
   Big with great thoughts and purpose high,
   He, too, has lived his day, and I,
The last and least, alone remain.

Onward, from Alp to Apennine!
   And soon across the distant sky
   Deep hues and deeper still we spy
Of that blue water's endless line.

By proud Genova's marbled way,
   And Pisa's famous tower, we gain
   Vald'arno's dear poetic plain,
Where sweet Firenze holds her sway.

VI.

O days of happiest memory past!
   O days twice dear when shared with thee!
   And yet once more to thee and me
One sacred scene, and that the last:

Together kneeling side by side,
   While hands on either head are laid,
   And holy prayers o'er each are said;
And from henceforth our ways divide.

But oh! too soon that course was done,
   That shone for thee with promise bright,
   Too soon the gathering shades of night
Had sunk upon thy work begun.

Too soon for those who mourn'd for thee,
—And who that knew yet mourn'd thee not?—
   For them too soon;—but thine the lot
Of God's own sons,—His Face to see.

                              1860.

HIGH FORCE.

WE stood beside the banks of Tees,
    Where, thundering down his dreadful way,
He flings his foam-shower to the breeze,
    And bathes the rocks with glittering spray.

We heard the voice of waters deep,—
    Not as when surges lash the shore,
And weary fitful pauses keep,—
    But one unbroken solemn roar:

We gazed, where the loud chiding flood
    Leaps from the tall cliff's rifted brow,
As earth-born giant, in wild mood,
    From castle-tower to earth below:

Above, bright clouds the sunbeams chased,
    And mountain-winds play'd soft and cool;
But dank beneath, and dimly traced,
    The storm-mist veil'd th' unfathom'd pool.

We gazed, while rapture still'd alarm,
    And half we thought, 'twere sweet to die
Lock'd in the torrent's mastering arm,
    The secrets of th' abyss to try.

Nor strange it seem'd, if Pagan wild,
    With earth and earth-born cares foredone,
Here deem'd some spirit, to mortals mild,
    Kept secret court in cavern lone.

And when more sadly sweet the fall
    Was heard beneath the soft moon-ray,
Mysterious harpings seem'd to call
    The toil-worn pilgrim soul away:

For where, but in such ceaseless flow,
    To whose loud chime the rock-vault rings,
Is seen so near on earth below
    The shadow of eternal things?

The restless motion, and the strife,
    The force that man can ne'er control,
O'ermastering all that here hath life,—
    It bows,—it melts,—it thrills the soul.

Dark stream, so fleet, so fugitive,
    So changeful, yet thy waves abide,
Arm'd with strong virtue to outlive
    Hard rock, and mountain's hoary pride:

Thy sound is of th' Eternal Power
    That bears this world of change along,
That at Creation's wondrous hour,
    When Angels woke the choral song,

Call'd thy rejoicing fountains forth,
    Unheard, unseen by man to glide;
But mountain warblers hail'd thy birth,
    And wild bees sipp'd that amber tide:

Then roll'd, as now, thy dark wave's shock:
    The trembling heart's deep silence hears,
In echoes from th' embattled rock,
    The voice of twice three thousand years.

1838.

A THOUGHT IN SUNSHINE.

There are, who love not summer bright,
   Who fly to arching groves or streams,
And view the Sun, as if with spite,
   "To tell him how they hate his beams."

Unwise!—when love or duty call,
   I'll court the heat and dusty way.
And where the full-orb'd glories fall
   Bathe in the golden showers of day.

I would not scorn the silent shade,
   Where Prayer may walk at eve or morn,
And Meditation lend her aid
   To hang sweet thoughts on every thorn:

But Rest is good when Toil is done:
   The evening hour, the calm of age,
Bring gladness after wages won
   In life's meridian pilgrimage.

The daily task I'll freely court
   While the bright Sun is mounting high,
And happy creatures glancing sport
   In joy beneath th' inspiring sky.

A THOUGHT IN SUNSHINE.

The weary limbs may slowly move,
   But the free soul shall taste that spring
Which eagle spirits drink above,
   The unsubdued of sight and wing.

August 11, 1853.

STANZAS ON LAMMAS DAY,

AUGUST 1.

WRITTEN FOR THE *Lyra Sanctorum.*

It is now sufficiently known that Lammas is a term derived from the Anglo-Saxon *Hlafmaes* or *Loaf-mass.* The day is duly honoured in the Poetical Menology of our Saxon forefathers and other ancient records; and it appears that loaves of the new corn, and sometimes offerings of new honey, were then presented in the churches, in imitation of the old Levitical offerings of the first-fruits (Deut. xxvi.) These gifts were given either to the priests or the poor, as seems intimated by the words of the Menology. "The weed-month," as August was called, "all summer bright bringeth to poor people the Loaf-mass day" (v. 265, *seq.*) In the Saxon monasteries the day seems to have been kept, as it was in the Eastern Church anciently, in memory of the Maccabees, and some records speak of it as also devoted to the honour of St. Germain. But the Lammas festival, as it was most purely national and of more general observance, has survived the remembrance of the other distinctions of the day.

A VISION fair of calm delight
    It was of old on Lammas morn,
When from low dale or wood-crown'd height,
    The chime of matin bells was borne,
Greeting true hearts in simple days
When Faith and Love kept equal ways.

At dawn, within some solemn fane,
    Where rose the shadowy central nave,
How brightly through the quarried pane
    The sun his orient greeting gave,
Gilding low roofs that spann'd above
God's home of humbleness and love.

The floor was throng'd with rustic souls
    Waiting to hear the voice of prayer,
And high were heap'd the bounteous doles
    Above and round God's Altar fair;
Where busy hands had come to rear
The first-fruits of the teeming year.

And now the priest had left his cell,
    And came with ancient book to pray,
And bless'd th' Archangel Panchiel*
    Who kept each evil bird away,

---

* This name, which appears to be the same with Peniel or Phanuel, "the Face of God," is taken from the old Durham Ritual, called *The Book of King Aldfrid;* where mention is made of this supposed angelic being as the protector of the fruits of

And worms, and mice, and such small deer,
That waste unseen the golden ear.

No fiend that walks in gloom had power
    To harm their fruitful furrowed land;
Soft winds had brought the timely shower,
    And slanting fell the levin-brand;
Nor whirlwind blast nor vapour's chill
Had struck the crops with nightly ill.

For why? a heavenly host was there,
    Led by their harnessed chief along,
Watching o'er earth, and floods, and air,
    Full four-and-forty thousand strong;
No evil thing could walk on ground,
Where those bright warders hovered round.

"Ye know," he said, "when last I bless'd
    The sparkling salt and water pure,
And flung them to Earth's open breast,
    That spell no goblin might endure,
But fled: as Raphael's spell could fray
The bridegroom-quelling Asmoday.

---

the earth, with a host of 44,000 angels under him. The custom of sprinkling salt and water hallowed for the purpose over the cultivated ground, as a symbol by which such spiritual aid was invoked, is also mentioned in the same Ritual. This ceremony most probably took place in Rogation week.

"Then let us bless the Holy One,
    Who by His Saints such help hath given,
And to our adjuration down
    Hath sent the denizens of heaven,
To shield each herb and seed and tree,
And flower that feeds the honey bee.

"And let us duly to Him bring
    The first-fruits of our land's increase,
The cell-work of the breathing Spring,
    The loaves, that, multiplied in peace,
Our store this day may spare to feed
The fainting sons of pain and need."

He bless'd the gifts with reverence meet,
    And silent for a space he bow'd:
Then rose the sound of harpings sweet,
    And choral voices, echoing loud
The massy pillar'd aisles along,
Pour'd forth the glad thanksgiving song.

Then near approach'd the pilgrim poor,
    The widow with her orphan child;
Grey sires, whose day of toil was o'er,
    Raised their pale eyes to heaven and smiled:
Glad hearts were theirs who bore away
The bounteous gifts of Lammas day.

But ere the summer's sun was seen
    High mounting to the point of noon,
Fast through the woodland alleys green
    The simple worshippers were gone,
Save where young boys retreating played
Like wild deer bounding through the shade.

'Tis past, that scene of other days;
    The simple tale we hear and smile;
We worship now in wiser ways;
    But say, does Mercy wake the while?
Does Love, as warm as theirs of yore
Now give to Heaven its golden store?

MY NEIGHBOUR'S LANDMARK.

FROM THE *Englishman's Magazine.*

The Cadi from the City's gate
    Goes forth in troubled mood:
Dark was his brow with cares of state
    As o'er the plain he rode.

The solemn mule that bore him forth
    That day was urged to speed
Unused to such degenerate birth
    Of tempest-footed steed.

He seeks beneath the dark hill's breast
    That palace rich and rare,
Where dwells in solace and in rest
    Great Abdalrahman's heir:

Where far below the mountain-pass
    Bright groves the courts embower;
Fair place! and fair its title was,
    The City of the Flower!

But where was now the home, that show'd
    What humble toil erewhile
Had tamed the wildness of the wood,
    And made the garden smile?

Where, free to hold its ancient space,
    A peasant's hearth might share
The pleasaunce of the glorious place
    With Abdalrahman's heir?

The Cadi gains the palace-door:
    A sack he hastes to fling
Across his shoulders, while the floor
    He treads to face the King:

"I ask a boon of little worth,—
    One boon my wish shall bound,—
One poor mule's burden of red earth
    From this enchanted ground."

Loud laugh'd the prince Alhakem; loud
    Was mirth in all the ring
Of wits and courtiers blithe of mood
    Who throng'd around the King.

"Let us walk forth;" he said; "my grooms,
    Who toil in sun or shade,
And dig the roots, or tend the blooms,
    Will bring the needful spade."

The Cadi led; and halted not,
    Till near the fountain's head,
Where late had stood the peasant's cot,
    His slow-paced beast he led.

There grew the flowers of odours sweet,
    As through the balmy air
They once were wont at eve to greet
    Their humbler master there.

But where the cottage walls of stone
    Erewhile were seen to rise,
A gay alcove now proudly shone
    To flout the summer skies.

" Here let us dig," the Cadi said :
    The sack was large and wide ;
But fast the mattock and the spade
    The busy delvers plied.

The task was done : " Now, faithful Lord,
    Once more thy servant prays,
Thy kingly help and strength afford,
    That sack from earth to raise."

" That sack of soil in all its weight
    To rear, and poise it true,
Sir Judge, I ween it were a feat
    For giant's strength to do."

" Ah King ! forgive thy faithful slave :
    Of all we do or dare
Far in a world beyond the grave
    The burden we must bear.

"If to a weight of earth so small
 Thy strength and spirit yield,
How wilt thou bear at doomsday all
 The poor man's plunder'd field?"

LAYS

OF

FAITH AND LOYALTY

" Of Honour with his spotless shield,
  And gentle Courtesy and Faith,
  Unchanged by sufferings, time, or death."
                                Marmion.

TO

JOSHUA WATSON, Esq.,

THROUGH LIFE

THE GENEROUS PATRON AND ADVOCATE

OF EDUCATION

IN THE SCHOOL OF FAITH AND LOYALTY,

THIS LITTLE VOLUME

IS GRATEFULLY AND AFFECTIONATELY

INSCRIBED.

ADVERTISEMENT.

IF it is true, as some one has said, that the wonders of History are greater than those of Fiction, and that stories of old times, however rudely told, are seldom listened to without pleasure; there may be a ground for hoping that the following pages will not be without acceptance among readers of that wondering and inquiring age for which they were principally intended. But the writer would not hold himself excused for adding a new book, even of so small a size, to the cheap literature of the day, had he not found reason to complain, that in many Historical Selections, or Historic Tales, put together for the young, in prose or verse, there is an absence of all moral purpose, a want of unity in the component parts, and of judgment in the choice of materials; so as to produce no effect beyond the amusement of the lower faculties of the mind, with things that scarcely deserve a more lasting remembrance.

In selecting the historical scenes which form the staple of the ballads contained in the present volume, the writer has confined himself to those which, whether of a lighter or more serious cast, seemed to have some bearing on the two best things that bind men to God and to each other,—Faith and Loyalty. And as the examples shown would be of no value, if they were not such as had appeared in real life, though they are taken from very different periods, from different ranks of life, and authorities of various character, it has been his aim to reject everything of a legendary kind, and to admit no incident which did not appear to be based essentially on historical truth.

I.

THE LITTLE MARTYR.

ROMANUS, a Deacon of the Church of Cæsarea in Palestine, suffered martyrdom at Antioch, in the persecution of Diocletian, A.D. 303. It appears from Eusebius that the Emperor Galerius was present at his trial, and directed a part of the cruel treatment, which he endured with wonderful fortitude and patience. The narrative in the following lines is taken from the account given by the Christian poet Prudentius of a remarkable incident which occurred at his martyrdom.

> 'TIS said, when good Romanus died
>   Beneath the Thracian's bitter sway,
> A little child the pagan's pride
>   Rebuked, and held his wrath at bay.
>
> " Grant me this test," the martyr cried,
>   By ruthless rods and scourges torn :
> " Let simple nature's voice decide
>   The truth your madness holds in scorn.
>
> " Choose out, from Antioch's crowded way,
>   Choose out the first young boy ye meet,
> And let his tongue unprompted say,
>   Before this frowning judgment-seat,

"Which faith to him may relish best;
  To hold one God with Christ His Son,
Or, what ye urge by ways unblest,
  A thousand forms of gods to own."

There stood a Roman matron by,
  And at her side a boy, whose years
Six summers scarce outran, whose eye
  No grief till now had dimm'd with tears.

"Ask him, and hear," the stern man said,
  Who sate on judgment's blood-stain'd throne;
"Ask as thou wilt;—our Jove to aid!
  Thy life by him is lost or won."

The question heard, the fair boy smiled:
  "Whate'er of God we think or say,
He must be One;—no little child
  Would dream of Heav'n's divided sway."

Amazed awhile the tyrant stood;
  Till re-collected powers of ill
Drove from his cheek the mantling blood
  Of generous shame that curb'd his will:

"'Tis practice all," in gloom he said:
  "Tell me, young boy, who taught this lore?"
The guileless child, of nought afraid,
  Smiled with such smile as Eden wore,

And, glancing at the matron's face,
"It was," he said, "the Spirit blest,
Who gave my mother dear such grace,
E'en while she fed me at her breast,

"That then of Christ I learnt to hear,
And sought to love Him for His love."
Alack! the puttock fierce was near,
That spares not e'en the nestling dove.

Swift at the bidding of their lord
The lictors seized that tender prey;
And swiftly sped the accursed word,
Which Mercy heard, and fled away:

"That godless mother,—let her see
The end of that most godless pain,
And let her child's quick scourgings be
As fire to pierce her inmost brain."

The scribes who watch'd what torture's power
Could do to work a soul's despair,—
High lords, from kingly hall or bower,
And bondsmen poor, stood weeping there.

'Tis said the very deathsmen wept,—
Hard souls, sworn foes to smile or tear;
Unbidden drops outstarting kept
Strange concord with their deeds of fear.

For from those little limbs, so frail,
    The sudden life-warm streams that flow'd,
So pure they were, so wondrous pale,
    Had more the hue of milk than blood.

Yet still the mother stood serene;
    No mortal pang her heart could move,
Stubborn to watch that deathful scene
    With love beyond a mother's love;

And bravely did the gallant boy
    Still watch his mother's radiant eye,
As though some treasured thought of joy
    Beam'd thence to check each shuddering sigh.

And now had torture done its worst;
    The fainting child, yet undismay'd,
In those fond arms that rock'd him first,
    For one brief pause of pain was laid.

"Mother," he said, "this parched lip,
    This gasping burning throat,—O tell,
May I not live one draught to sip,—
    One,—from our own bright sparkling well?"

"My child, the Well prepared for thee
    With life and health unchanging flows;
Let thy soul thirst that Well to see;
    Forget thy present iron woes.

" Now must thou drink that cup of doom,
    The babes of Bethlehem drank whilere ;
Rough is the edge of martyrdom,
    But, past, eternal sweets are there."

She bore him where the swordsman stood,
    Prepared to sever life's frail thread :
So, in the arms of Abel good,
    Ere yet by envious Cain he bled,

Perchance the firstling of his flock,
    More pure than all the rest, was borne :
She dallied not with death's fierce shock,
    Nor stay'd her life's sweet hope to mourn ;

But with one kiss resign'd her charge :
    " Go, sweetest babe : henceforth for thee
No need of prayer : but, once at large
    In that blest presence, pray for me !"

II.

ALARIC THE GOTH.

THE incidents related in the following ballad are all recorded in the historians of the time; but more particularly by the Christian historians, Socrates, B. vii. c. 10, and Sozomen, B. ix. c. 6. 9. The concluding portion is almost a version of the narrative of Orosius, B. vii. c. 39.

'TWAS a sight to rouse from sleep
Spirits of the viewless deep,
Brenn, and hardy Hannibal,
And Rome's ancient foemen all,
    When fierce Alaric's trumpet-tone
    Called the hour of vengeance on,
    And the Goth to Rome was gone.

Foremost in the van he came,
Heart of steel, and eye of flame,
Gay with gold, as he would ride
But to seek a courtly bride;
    Gay with gold his charger shone,
    Large of limb, and strong of bone,
    Meet for Terror's dazzling throne.

There, as war his pastime were,
Oft he hurl'd aloft his spear,
And, with fleet horse wheeling round,
Caught it ere it came to ground,
   Bending back, or stooping down.
   Lithe as dancer in saloon,
   Where the winged shaft had flown.*

Senators from Rome drew nigh,
Peace with love or gold to buy:
" Peace we ask: but ere we fall,
Myriads wait to man the wall;
   Die we will with armour on,
   Ere our Empire's fence of stone
   Shall by vagrant Goths be won."

---

* The Byzantine historian, Procopius, gives this picture of the Gothic King Totila, just before his last battle with Narses: B. iv., c. 31. "He did not shun the observation of the enemy. For he was clad in a suit of armour lavishly bespangled with gold, and an uncommon quantity of crimson hung from the harness of his horse, from his head-piece, and his spear, giving him a very kingly appearance. He was mounted upon a strong and tall horse, and wheeling round and round as he rode, often threw his quivering spear aloft, and caught it as it descended; then he would change it from hand to hand, and shewed his dexterity by leaning his body far back, or stooping down, and again from side to side, as if he had been well taught all dancing exercises from his youth."

Grimly smiled the hardy Goth:
"Thickest grass gives easiest swath;
In the city's crowded throng
Soonest reaps war's faulchion strong."
 Loud again the trumpet's tone
 Spake that hope of peace was none:
 And the Goth to Rome is gone.

Next there came an aged monk;
Low at Alaric's feet he sunk:
"Warrior, dread the day of doom;
Spare to glut thy rage on Rome.
 Think what penance can atone
 For the deeds that must be done,
 Ere thou climb the Cæsars' throne."

For a moment Alaric heard,
As with inward anger stirr'd:
But he smooth'd his ruffled brow,
And his words were calm and low:
 "Father, let the guilty groan;
 For, believe, a mightier One
 Brings this day of vengeance on:

"There is One, Who, day and night,
Stands before my soul's clear sight,
Speaks, and says, '*The hour is come,
Go and sack the guilty Rome.*'"

Then again the trumpet's tone
Spake, that hope of peace was none;
And the Goth to Rome is gone.

Now in Rome fierce discord raves,
Wild the strife of lords and slaves,
When sharp danger came to bear
Hope to these, to those despair:
    Blest that realm, and blest alone,
    Where the rich and poor, as one,
    Know the public weal their own!

Rome's sad sons of want and woe
Deem'd each child of wealth their foe,
And in secret league they wait
To unbar the city's gate:
  "Let the valiant Goth come on;
    Then oppression's task is done,
    Bonds are broken, freedom won."

Sorcerers by the Senate stood,
Bold to curse the Christian's God,
Tuscan augurs grim, who vow'd
To compel Jove's thunder-cloud,
    Let but sacrifice atone
    For the wrongs by Christians done
    To his Capitolian throne.

But with patient mien the while,
To Saint Peter's solemn aisle
Throng'd the poor of Christ to pray:
Maidens meek in sad array,
    Hoary age and youth are gone;
    Low they kneel on floor of stone,
    Pleading for a realm undone.

Short was now the respite given:
Lo! the gates asunder riven;
And, as levin-brand that shrouds
Brightest flash in darkest clouds,
    Ere the night's last watch was gone,
    Flashing roll'd the squadrons on;
    Rome at early dawn was won.

"Liegemen, hasten to the spoil,"
Alaric cried, "the prize of toil;
But God's holy homes forbear,
Touch not one who shelters there;
    Let not age unpitied groan,
    Let no maid or matron's moan
    Make just God our cause disown."

Then arose the loud acclaim;
Wild blue eyes were lit with flame;
At their monarch's kindling words
Waved the banners, clash'd the swords;

Twice ten thousand hearts, as one,
Beat accordant to the tone,
Joyous in the conquest won.

Rome, sad Rome, what fate is hers!
Temples, porches, theatres,
Towers strong, and pillars high,
Rich with storied imagery,
   Arches reared with sculptured stone,
   Shall their place no more be known,
   In one mighty wreck o'erthrown?

Who can stay fierce Alaric? No man;
But there stands a lonely woman,*
Feeble seems she, old, and poor,
Waiting at a low-arch'd door.
   "Sigismer, my comrade boon,
   Go, accost that ancient crone,
   And dispatch her business soon;"

---

* She appears to have been a devout sister and servant of the church of St. Peter's, as Phœbe was at Corinth (Rom. xvi. 1), and was, perhaps, entrusted with the care of the sacred vessels in virtue of that office. St. Augustine confirms the account of Orosius, in his Treatise on the City of God, B. i., c. 4. And it was this narrative which made our own excellent King Alfred, in his epitome of Orosius, to call Alaric "the most Christian and the mildest king."

Alaric spoke. Count Sigismer,
With half-gay, half-serious air,
Bow'd him to that beldame poor,
Waiting at her low-arch'd door:
 "Gentle lady, thou art one
  Whom the Gothic sword hath won,
  Thou, and all thou call'st thine own:

"But for thee, may peace still bless
Thy long age's loneliness;
War, just war, may strike the strong,
Feeble eld it may not wrong:
 But we ask thy gold alone;
  Gold, and gold's pale sister wan,
  Speed the sons of conquest on."

"Gold I have," the beldame said,
And within the door display'd
Service rich of vases rare,
Golden lamp, and chalice fair;
 All beyond the threshold stone
  Bright the vaulted chamber shone,
  Guarded by that feeble crone.

For a space in mute surprise
Fix'd the Goth his wond'ring eyes:
But when he would seize the prey,
Thus her warning voice said nay:

"Not for thy bright habergeon,
  Or thy dragon-crested cone,
  Dare to cross the threshold-stone.

"Lo! those censers, made to bear
  Odours sweet to waft with pray'r,
  Lamps, in holy Peter's choir
  Set to burn with hallow'd fire,
    Cups, for blood that could atone
    For all earth's dread malison,
    Blood that Heaven's sweet pardon won.

"Feeble, old, and poor am I;
  Arm of strength I may not try;
  But if thou this deed shalt dare,
  Be the following curse thy care."
    Fast, with mutter'd orison,
    Left the Goth that arch of stone,
    And to Alaric's side is gone.

What a change o'er Alaric pass'd!
Loud he blew his trumpet-blast,
Calling to his royal side
Many a warrior scatter'd wide:
  "Render first to God His Own;
  Take those vessels one by one,
  And to Peter's Church lead on."

On their heads his warriors bore
All that consecrated store,
While around a guard array'd
Shoulder'd each his naked blade:
    But not yet enough was done;
    Once again the trumpet's tone
    Made the monarch's purpose known.

"Christian, born at Rome, or Goth,
Not for thee this hour of wrath:
Come, as moves our pomp along,
Come with chaunt and holy song:
    For our trumpet's solemn tone
    Bids divided hearts be one;
    Let the faithless mourn alone."

Thick as flock the driven deer
To the pass of safety near,
Pagans back with Christians turn'd,
Shelter'd by the Name they scorn'd:
    Fast as came that concourse on,
    Gothic swords to guard them shone:
    Who should seek to make them known?

Such was Alaric's proudest day:
Let the sons of glory say,
When was victory's full career
Stay'd, like this, at age's prayer?

Like a Christian champion,
He to gain his crown pass'd on :
Christ was served, while Rome was won.

III.

THE CALIPH AND HIS PHYSICIAN.

The Caliph Motavakel, who reigned at Bagdad from A.D. 847-861, was a dissolute and cruel prince, who persecuted both the Jews and Christians who were subject to his dominion, and was equally tyrannical to those of his own household. Hence his son, Montasser, was provoked to a fearful act of vengeance; for he is said to have shed his father's blood, and so ascended the vacant throne; which, however, he held only for six months, distracted by the agonies of remorse. His death was hastened by a remarkable incident. He was standing by while some attendants were unrolling a piece of ancient tapestry, which represented a horseman with a crown upon his head, round which was a scroll inscribed with Persian characters. Being ignorant of the language, Montasser asked the meaning from an interpreter, who, after some delay and hesitation, at length with pale looks and a faltering tone, read the inscription as follows:—" I am Siroes, the son of Chosroes; I slew my father, and retained the royal dignity but six months." The shock of these words was so great to the wounded conscience of Montasser, that he died shortly afterwards; a victim to the terrors of Divine vengeance.

THE CALIPH AND HIS PHYSICIAN.

The narrative contained in the following lines is taken from the History of Abulfaragius, the Christian historian of the East, of whom a short account is given in Dr. Hook's Eccl. Biography. It occurred in the reign of Motavakel, who is the Caliph here alluded to. The name of the Christian Physician was, according to Abulfaragius, Honain, perhaps an Arabic corruption of Johannes, or John.

THE Caliph, in a garden fair,
 Beneath a bright alcove,
At eve drank in the perfumed air,
 Breath'd from the lilac grove;

And at his feet a learned leech
 Beguiled the twilight hour,
Whose chemic art each use could teach
 Of mineral, herb, and flower.

A Greek he was of Christian race,
 Who ventured far to roam;
For Science gives in every place
 Her favourite sons a home.

Yet safer oft midst rocks and waves
 The bark its course may steer,
Than tongue of truth, that boldly braves
 A despot's wayward ear.

THE CALIPH AND HIS PHYSICIAN.

" Physician," the dark Caliph said,
"Such skill is sure thine own,
As in our holy books 'tis read
To Solomon was known:

" Thy limbeck can each juice refine
Of plant, and herb, and tree;
The subtle genii of the mine
Have cull'd their spells for thee:

" Then tell me by what secret way
I may despatch my foe,
And no detected sign betray
The charm that works him woe."

Long silent sate the gentle leech,
His hand upon his brow:
Ah, well, he thought, did Science teach
The Coan sage his vow!*

---

* Hippocrates of Cos, the father of physicians, places in the front of his treatise an oath or vow to be taken by the student of medicine, that he will never use his knowledge for purposes of harm to any one. It is well known that our countryman, the famous John Hunter, left it on record that he had discovered a poison of such a subtle nature, that, lest it should be abused to the destruction of human life, he determined the knowledge should die with him. The conduct of this eminent man may serve to illustrate the principle which swayed the physician Honain.

Why did I stray from pleasant Greece,
    And Freedom's mountain air,
To dwell amidst the foes of peace,
    And tempt the serpent's lair?

God and good Saints be now my speed!
    For earthly hope is none:
And, but Heav'n help me at my need,
    My art and life are done.

Then starting from that painful trance,
    He meekly rais'd his head,
And scann'd the tyrant's piercing glance,
    But not a word he said.

What word might slave to despot say,
    Who with a look might quell;
With whom to hear was to obey,
    To question, to rebel?

Again the Caliph spoke: "Take heed,
    And let thy speech be true;
For well I ween, thy skill can read
    What subtlest craft may do."

"What *craft* may do, I know not well,"
    The leech did mildly say,
"But my true art life's citadel
    Must succour, not betray."

In wrath the Caliph smote his hands;
    His eunuchs, one and all,
Came flocking fast in grisly bands
    Forth from the palace-hall.

"Seize ye that slave; it is our doom,"
    The tyrant sternly cried,
"And bear him where the dungeon's gloom
    May tame his stubborn pride.

"To-morrow be the secret said,
    Disclosed the lore I crave;
Or deep shall be his evening bed
    In Tigris' rolling wave."

"Despair thy dooms," the leech replied;
    "Though life's last hope be flown:
My faith and art that lore will hide
    For evermore unknown.

"My faith, that bids me seek his weal,
    Who most desires my ill;
My art, ordain'd life's griefs to heal;
    To save, and not to kill."

Dark passions shook the Caliph's frame;
    And heav'n and hell within
Were struggling, till the purer flame
    Rebuked his sullen sin.

"Enough;" he said, "thy truth is proved;
  And honour'd be the faith,
That for the mercy that it loved
  Endured to look on death.

"Bring forth bright robes, and on his hand,
  Be set our signet-ring;
'Tis meet the bold for truth should stand
  In council with a king."

IV.

SAINT EDMUND OF EAST ANGLIA.

THE earliest historical account of King Edmund, the royal Saint of Bury, is that of Abbo of Fleury, one of the learned friends of Archbishop Dunstan, who presided for some time as Abbot of Ramsey, in Huntingdonshire, then newly founded, A.D. 960, by Oswald, Bishop of Worcester. From his account, more than one Anglo-Saxon homily was supplied with such particulars of the King's life and character, and of his remarkable death, as it would be unreasonable scepticism to set down as merely fictitious. Abbo received these particulars from the mouth of St. Dunstan; and Dunstan professed to relate them, as he had himself heard them in his youth, from an officer, called "King Edmund's sword-bearer," one, probably, whose office had been to bear the sword of state in the royal presence on days of public ceremony, and who was then living at a very advanced age in the court of King Athelstan. This is not beyond the limits of historical probability, if we recollect that it was usual for well-born youths to go to the ancient German or Saxon courts at the age of thirteen or fourteen, to find a place among the attendants on royalty. (*See* Tacitus, *Germ.* c. 13, Eddius,

Vit. S. Wilfrid, c. 2.) Supposing the sword-bearer to have been a boy of that age in A.D. 870, the date assigned by the earliest authorities for the death of Edmund, it is quite credible that he might have been living between sixty and seventy years later, when Dunstan, who was born in A.D. 925, appears to have gone to the court of Athelstan.

There are many contradictions, which modern inquiry has not cleared up, between the Danish and English accounts of the fate of Reyner Lodbroke, the father of the five brave sons who so long disputed the possession of England with the great Alfred. It is merely necessary at present to say that the writer has chosen to follow the account of several of our own ancient chroniclers, in preference to that of *Lodbroker Quida*, or Death-Song of Lodbroke, and other Scandinavian authorities, which have been preferred by the ingenious M. Lamé Fleury, in his interesting juvenile *Histoire du Moyen Age*, and by other recent historians, and which attribute the hero's death to Ælla, the usurper of Northumbria, and of St. Cuthbert's patrimony at Crayke.

It seems probable, from the accounts of Matt. Westminster and Fordun, that the great Danish invasion, which began in A.D. 866, was reinforced by a new armament in A.D. 870. This second force landed in the spring or summer on the coast of Scotland, and having slain in battle Constantine, son of Kenneth

MacAlpine, marched southwards through Mercia into East Anglia. Here, after a hard fight with the natives near Thetford, they were joined by a detachment of the first army, which came by sea from York, and so became masters of the country. The account in the Saxon Homilies speaks only of an army coming by sea, and it seems, by other accounts, that the East Anglians were taken by surprise, as they had four years earlier made peace with the first invaders, whose point of attack had been the kingdom of Northumbria.

King Edmund fell on the twentieth day of November, A.D. 870; and all our old writers who enter into particulars represent his death as an act of voluntary suffering; that he refused to fly when flight was in his power, believing that his death would save his people from further extremities of war, and counting it an act of impiety in a Christian prince to hold his crown as a subject of a pagan superior. For this his name was honoured through many generations of those who came after. A stately abbey was reared by the bounty of Edmund the Elder, and enriched by gifts from many kings and princes on the spot where his bones were laid to rest. His character, as was natural, was highly reverenced by merciful and gentle monarchs, such as Edward the Confessor and Henry VI.; and his praises were sung by Lydgate and other old poets of our native land.

The abbey, for certain reasons of state, was destroyed by Henry VIII., together with the other great abbeys; but there is yet a college at Oxford which is called after the royal martyr, and, among other parish churches, one in London, of which her Majesty the Queen and the Archbishop of Canterbury are patrons. His name remains in our Calendar on the day of his martyrdom; and he is altogether one of those for whom we may suppose the gentle Muse of Spenser pleaded against the Puritan :

> " The hilles, where dwelled holy Sainets,
> I reverence and adore,
> Not for themselves, but for the Sainets
> Which han bene dead of yore :
> Shepherds they weren of the best,
> And lived in lowly leas :
> And sith their soules be now at rest,
> Why do we them dis-ease?"

When, on the death of Hardacnute, Magnus the Good, King of Norway, had succeeded to the throne of Denmark, he sent a message to Edward the Confessor, to say that, as the heir of Hardacnute, he considered himself entitled to England also. The Confessor, after explaining his hereditary right, concluded his answer thus : "While I live I will not renounce my title. If King Magnus come hither with an army, I will gather no army against him; but he shall only get possession of England when he has taken my life." On hearing this answer Magnus gave up his designs on England : "I think it wisest and best," he said, "that each of us should keep the kingdom that God has given us."—(*Snorro's Chronicle*, vol. ii. p. 398. Mr. Laing's Transl.) Edward's answer strongly illustrates the history of St. Edmund; and no doubt the waste of much blood and treasure might be prevented by such a spirit of patriotic self-devotion in Christian kings.

Part I.

Voyage of Regner Lodbroke.

Woe worth the day, may Saxon say,
    When o'er the salt sea-foam,
With eastern gale, that breedeth bale,
    The Dane went forth to roam.

Woe worth the day, in Yare's broad bay,
    When first the Saxon found
The stranger's bark from waters dark
    Escaped to English ground.

But double woe to him who dared
    The stranger's rights to spurn,
Who struck the breast in friendship bared,
    Woe to the traitor, Berne.

For not in guise of pirate war
    That lonely wanderer came;
No raven-banner stream'd afar
    O'er men of steel and flame.

It was when Norway's realm of rock
    Doth court brief summer's smile,
And summer birds unnumber'd flock
    To northern cove and isle;

When ocean-caves, the sea-fowl's haunt,
    Such clangs of music bear,
As though wild Nature raised her chaunt
    In vaulted temple there:

Bold Reyner launch'd his bark at morn,
    His hawk was on his hand;
Lightly his little sail was borne
    Around each jutting strand;

And lightly soar'd the bird on high,
    And downward stoop'd to gain
The gannet, or the golden eye,
    That dived beneath the main.

The morn was bright, the hearts were light,
    That hail'd that morning ray;
But waters dark roll'd round his bark
    Before the closing day;

And far from shore, in spite of oar,
    The wind that breedeth bane,
The felon wind to life unkind,
    Hath borne the noble Dane.

Long may his royal dame keep ward
    On Jutland's sounding shore,
And look to see her jocund lord;
    But he returns no more:

For far away, in Yare's broad bay,
    The Saxon carle hath found
The stranger's bark from waters dark
    Escaped to English ground.

I wot not, I, how oft the night
    Give place to star of morn,
While o'er the loud flood's weltering might
    His giddy bark was borne;

But, all unharm'd by wildest wave,
    On Yare's warm bank he lay;
Kind hearts and boon his welcome gave
    At Reedham's hamlet grey.

His hawk so good to fresh green wood
    Is free again to roam,
And from her wings, as up she springs,
    She shakes the salt sea-foam.

But when her master's call she hears,
    She perches on his hand:
And Reyner now would meet his peers,
    The nobles of the land.

To saintly Edmund's court they ride,
    By Waveney's silent stream,
When now the day's last lustre died,
    And rose the pale moonbeam.

There rests the Dane with toil forespent,
    A pious prince's care,
Whose faith receives such guests as sent
    Like angels, unaware:

"Strange wonders on the loud sea-flood,"
    He said, "our guest hath known;
But He whose spirits guard the good
    Thus marks him for His Own.

"Our holy clerks, with gentlest lore,
    Shall melt his pagan pride,
Till Faith and Hope their golden door
    For him shall open wide."

Ah, woe to him whose envy dared
    His lord's behest to spurn;
Who pierced the breast in friendship bared,
    Woe to the traitor, Berne! *

---

* Berne, the murderer of Reyner Lodbroke, was the King's falconer, or master of the hounds; and he is supposed to have committed the foul deed out of envy against one who excelled him in his own craft.

The summer eve hath past away,
    And autumn blasts are chill:
The leaves fall sear from bush and spray
    On every holt and hill:

The hunters rouse; but where the Dane,
    Who led the chase at morn?
His hawk that never soar'd in vain,
    Why droops she on the thorn?

His good greyhound, so light of bound,
    Why quails his courage now?
Foul treason's blade his lord hath laid
    Beneath the greenwood bough.

Woe worth the day, may Saxon say,
    The child unborn may rue
That traitor's blow, which bred all woe
    To loving hearts and true.

Part II.

Invasion of the Danes.

Our simple Saxon ancestors,
   Their faith was firm and strong,
That heaven would change fixed nature's course,
   Ere truth should suffer wrong:

And when the solemn priest had bless'd
   Hot wave or glowing steel,
That guiltless hand might bide the test,
   Which only guilt would feel:

For secret spirits waited by,
   If innocence were there,
To bid the cauldron's fury die,
   And quench the molten share.

But now for Berne another test
   The wise in council find:
"Let him, too, try the broad sea's breast,
   The sport of wave and wind:

"Safe in that boat did Reyner float;
   Such grace to him was given:
And this false groom may brave his doom,
   If he have peace with heaven."

Alas! the felon lives, dismiss'd
    From fear and danger free:
Soft western gales his white sail kiss'd,
    And curl'd the laughing sea;

And that strange bark, from Ocean dark
    Borne back to Denmark came;
And Berne's false tale hath arm'd for bale
    The sons of steel and flame.

They come to wreak a father's wrong;
    Hinguar with heart of pride,
And Hubba fierce, and Guttorm strong,
    In vengeance o'er the tide.

The swineherd led his charge from mast,
    Ere evening wolves might roam,
Where stood God's house upon the waste,
    Saint Bennet's of the Holme;*

His quick eye watch'd the gathering gloom
    Beneath the branching tree,
Nor mark'd where fiercer spoilers come,
    The war-wolves of the sea.

---

* This monastery stood in the parish of Wickmere, near Aylsham, not very far from King Edmund's hall at Halesdon. It was utterly destroyed by the Danes at this invasion; but was restored before the Norman conquest, and remained till the dissolution.

Saint Bennet's sons, with anthem clear,
    Sung to the Trinal Light,
Pray'd help in hours of darkness drear,
    From phantoms of the night.

Again, at midnight's iron chime,
    Arose those monks to prayer;
But ere they met at song of prime,
    A house of dead was there.

The loud stag called to deer and fawn,
    Ere, brightening into day,
On Halesdon's wood-encircled lawn
    The twilight shadows lay:

The saintly king was roused, and forth
    He gazed from lattice high;
Wild fires were dancing in the north,
    And redly glared the sky.

Short pause for question,—ere the sun
    Unveil'd the dewy mead,
Came hurrying posts of slaughter done,
    Quick voice and flying steed:

Then sad and slow, an old, old man,[*]
    On weary palfrey borne;
His reverend face was pale and wan,
    His mitred locks were torn:

---

[*] Humbert, Bishop of Elmham, who, according to Matt.

Breathless and faint, in piteous mood
    His lips their tale prolong :
"Heaven's vengeance for Earl Reyner's blood,
    O King, is wondrous strong.

"The traitor Berne,—too plain his guilt,—
    O day of grief and tine !
That felon life, by thee unspilt,
    Returns to strike at thine.

"Earl Reyner's sons lead on the war,—
    Good King, thy friends are slain ;
Fly, while the pitying morning-star
    Beams eastward o'er the plain."

Scarce had he ceased, that man in years,
    Bow'd down with woe and toil,
When, following close, a stranger fierce
    Rode o'er the sounding soil :

"To thee, Sir King, short rede I bring :
    King Hinguar's might is nigh :
Canst thou withstand his conquering hand ?
    Thy choice is, Yield, or die :

Westminster, was slain by the Danes, with King Edmund. He must have been a very aged man, as he had been Bishop more than fifty years.

Yield, nor withhold thy hoarded gold,
    And homage meetly done,
He bids thee live, and back will give
    The realm his sword hath won."

The King to aged Humbert spake:
    "Good father, sorely tried,
Who didst thy needful couch forsake,
    So far by night to ride;

"And thou, the Dane's proud messenger,
    Untrain'd in Christian lore:
Be sure, life's gift unlovely were,
    When life's best cause is o'er.

"For my loved thanes my heart is woe,
    For wife and helpless bairn,
Whom, by fell pagans' wrath laid low,
    No message did forewarn:

"And shall I from the remnant flee,
    Nor heed their suffering cry?
Less meet it were, that they for me,
    Than I for them should die.

"Vicegerents of the Eternal King.
    Whom heavenly hosts obey,
Shall kings not dread His doom, who fling
    Their priceless charge away?

"Come death, come life, farewell to strife;
  With no blood-guilty hand,
For God's sweet love, who reigns above,
  And my dear fatherland,

"Here will I bide whate'er betide,
  Resistance offering none;
Yet none shall see my bended knee,
  Save Heaven's blest Lord alone."

He stood within his palace-hall,
  His battle-bow unstrung,
His spear and shield upon the wall,
  In guise of peace, up-hung;

As though that voice were in his ear,
  Spoke by the lifeful Word,
That they whose wrath the sword shall bear,
  Shall perish by the sword.

He stood,—he bore death's agony,
  The worst that hate could bring,
Resolved as he had lived, to die,
  A Saint,—a Christian King.

Think gently of our fathers' faith,
  If for a soul like this
They deem'd strange wonders after death
  Bespoke his spirit's bliss;

How voices through the woodland maze
    Were echoing far and near,
To guide amidst those tangled ways
    The friends that loved him dear;

And how the grim grey wolf outspread,
    By heaven withheld from prey,
Sate guardian of that holy head,
    And chased all harms away.

Though long undone his shrine of stone
    Fair may his memory stand,
Martyr of love to God above,
    And his dear fatherland.

V.

A STORY OF SAINT OLAVE.

This story of St. Olave, who was king of Norway while Ethelred, and afterwards Canute, reigned in England, A.D. 1014–1030, is related by Snorro in his *Chronicle of the Kings of Norway*, vol. ii. p. 297 of Mr. Laing's Translation. It is also selected by modern writers on the Sacred Antiquities of Sweden and Norway, who wisely reject other stories of a more legendary character, which have been invented in later times to magnify St. Olave. See John Vastovius in his *Vitis Aquilonia*, and Benzelius's note, p. 28, and Annot, p. 23, ed. Upsal. 1768.

Whatever may be thought of the act recorded, which may not accord with more refined times and manners, the delicacy of feeling which led the royal saint rather to inflict pain upon himself than offend the weak conscience of a poor and more ignorant fellow-Christian, is surely worthy of this brief record.

It was the Sabbath evening hour,
 The calm of hearts believing,
The saintly King in silent bower
 Sweet fancy's chain sat weaving.

In his left hand a staff of pine
    His quiet grasp enfolded;
His right, a blade both bright and fine,
    With which the staff he moulded.

An honest thrall, who waited by,
    His lord's behest observing,
All heedless of his reverie,
    From duty deem'd him swerving:

At length, his courage rising higher,
    In tone of simple sorrow
He said, "It will be Monday, Sire,
    If Heaven so please, to-morrow."

"Gramercy, friend," the King replied,
    "The fault was unintended;
But fitting penance shall abide
    The hand that so offended."

He grasp'd the shavings great and small
    As close as hand could handle,
Then bade the kind-reproving thrall
    To bring a lighted candle;

And on his much-enduring palm
    He let them burn together,
His visage all unmoved and calm
    As Norway's summer weather.

Whene'er St. Olave's church I see,—
    Let scorners call it folly,—
This tale shall be a hint to me
    To keep the Sabbath holy.

VI.

THE CID AND DON MARTIN OF ASTURIA.

THIS tale is taken from the Chronicle of the Cid, § 36, 37. The conduct of the old warrior in this instance bears a striking resemblance to that of the gallant Lord Dundee, as related by other Scottish historians and by Sir Walter Scott in his *History of Scotland*, chap. lvi. But that case had a more unfortunate and tragical conclusion.

WHEN before Valencia's city,
    Ere the leaguer'd Moors would yield,
Lay the noble Cid Ruy Diaz
    Watching in the tented field:

To his camp at early morning,
    In the pause of hardy fight,
Mounted on a fiery jennet
    Rode a young and comely knight.

Thus he spoke to bold Rodrigo:
    "From Asturia's mountain-brow
I have sought thee, as the pilgrim
    Seeks the temple of his vow.

"From the Pass of Covadonga
  Cradle of the might of Spain,
In whose heights the mountain-eagle
  Holds his unapproach'd domain,

"Moved by tidings of thy valour
  I have led my followers on;
Nobly am I born, my name is
  Martin, Count Pelayo's son.

"Glad from far I hail'd thy banner,
  By the morning breezes fann'd.
Take my gage: I pledge my service,
  Heart to heart and hand to hand."

Doubtfully the champion scann'd him;
  Tall he was, and large of limb;
But his tongue was all too fluent,
  And his beard was all too trim.

Much suspected good Rodrigo,
  When to battle he would ride,
It was but some knight of ladies
  Who had mounted by his side.

True his thought: for, ere the onslaught
  Of the Christian on the Moor,
On his courser gaily prancing
  Burnish'd arms Don Martin wore;

But the din of Moorish tambours,
　　And the swarthy warriors' glare,—
Did they fright Don Martin's courser?
　　Horse and man, he vanish'd there.

Back he fled; and with discretion,
　　Venturous valour's better part,
In his tent, till fight was ended,
　　Hid the throbbings of his heart.

Till the Cid, at noon returning
　　With the dye of carnage red,
Bathed his hands, all foul and weary
　　With the blood of Paynims dead.

Then the feast was spread before him,
　　As was wont, on tables twain,
One to grace the gallant Captain,
　　One, his knights, the flower of Spain.

None but knights of hardiest daring,
　　Well approved, of courage strong,
Tried in many a field of danger,
　　Might appear those ranks among:

" Every man must do his duty,"
　　So the Cid his order gave,
" Ere he dine with Alvar Fanez
　　At the table of the brave."

Little deem'd the trembling novice,
 In the tumult of that day,
That his captain's eye beheld him
 When he turn'd him from the fray:

Soon he bathed his hands in water,
 Though the need, I ween, was small;
And his seat with Alvar Fanez
 Took amidst those warriors tall.

When the Cid espied that rashness,
 From his stool in haste he flew:
"Those are braver men, Don Martin,
 Braver men than I, or you:

"Come and seat thee at my table,
 And with me the banquet share."
Little dream'd the simple novice
 What should next await him there.

Braver man than good Rodrigo
 Never held the name of brave;
But no less his generous pity,
 Wavering worth to spare and save.

When the brief repast was ended,
 And the assembled knights were gone,
Thus bespoke the good Rodrigo
 Martin, Count Pelayo's son:

DON MARTIN OF ASTURIA.

There was anger mix'd with sadness
    In the warrior's solemn tone,
While he spoke, as speak the noble,
    To the offender's ear alone:

"Can it be that thou, Don Martin,
    Born as thou art born, should'st fly?
Hadst thou fall'n, it were thine honour
    In the battle-field to die.

"Wilt thou tell me that the Paynims
    In a mighty throng came round?
Many a gallant knight was near thee,
    Bravely they maintain'd their ground.

"Seek a house of still religion,
    There thy vows may yet be true;
There thou may'st do God that service,
    Which in arms thou canst not do.

"Or if now thine ebbing spirits
    Thou canst summon to their flow,
Mount and ride with me at even,
    Go where honour bids thee go.

"At my side perchance thy terror
    Less may move thee in the fray;
But the brave must stand unshaken
    With a thousand foes at bay.

"So farewell till then, Don Martin;
  Till thy fault amended be,
Till thou hast retrieved thy honour,
  Thou must dine no more with me."

Sorely shent Don Martin parted,
  Pierced with shame and deep dismay;
Like the jay of borrow'd feathers
  Stripp'd, he shrunk from sight of day.

But the generous chieftain's chiding
  Not in vain his soul had moved;
Most of all this hope assured him,
  That his worth might still be proved.

Soon again the Cid has summon'd
  To assail Valencia's towers,
And the Moors a desperate sally
  Made with their united powers.

Who was then of knights the foremost
  In war's stern career to run?
Who unhorsed the foremost Paynim?
  Martin, Count Pelayo's son.

Strangely were the Moors confounded,
  Back they turned with sudden dread;
"Eblis, sure, hath sent that demon
  From the caverns of the dead."

Like a flock of sheep fast crowding
    To the entrance of the fold,
So the Moors retired before him
    To regain Valencia's hold.

Then not Mars himself could scorn him,
    Who such dangerous fame had woo'd,
From his wrists above his elbows
    His strong arms were bathed in blood.

Lovingly the Cid embraced him,
    Waiting on his homeward way:
" Martin, son of brave Pelayo,
    Thou hast proved thy birth this day.

" 'Tis too low for thy brave merit
    At my board to sit by far;
Go and sit with Alvar Fanez,
    My first brother in the war;

" And with those brave knights, his comrades,
    Born in feats of arms to shine;
Well-esteem'd ones, meet companions
    For a generous soul like thine."

From that day the Asturian novice
    Never quail'd in fight again;
Well he proved that generous chiding
    Had not pierced his heart in vain.

Well he proved how true the proverb,
 By old wisdom sung or said :
Choose a goodly tree for shelter,
 Thou shalt find a goodly shade.

VII.

ST. BERNARD'S YOUNGER BROTHER.

The anecdote, and its sequel, here related, will be familiar to those who have read almost any life of St. Bernard. It is told on the authority of his friend and contemporary, who was also his first biographer, William de St. Thierry.

When shall the world again behold
    The souls, who with undazzled eye
Turn'd from Grim Mammon's heaps of gold,
    And, meditating but to die,
Sought the cool vale, whose waters bless
The low-built cell of humbleness?

'Twas thus four sons of one old sire
    Went forth from one paternal hall
(Such zeal could Bernard's call inspire),
    To seek the still Cistercian wall;
Together from the pleasant door
They turn'd them, to return no more.

Their sire, long tried in deeds of arms,
    Had train'd them for the tented field,
And proudly seen in war's alarms
    How well they stood with sword and shield;

But now fast fell a father's tears,
To lose the solace of his years.

Fast fell his tears; his voice was faint;
  But his old heart was firm and strong:
"God's will be done! my buried saint
  Had bless'd your choice, and grief were wrong.
Though lost are five, young Nivard yet
Attends my age, else desolate."

Through Dijon's town they took their way;
  Each well-remember'd face they greet:
Till where a little troop at play
  Came shouting down the noisy street,
A gentle school-boy hurrying by
Paused where he met his brother's eye.

"Nivard," said Guy, the eldest born,
  "Farewell, and God's best benison
Be thine, implored each eve and morn
  By us, who leave thee for thine own
Our heritage by dale and hill,
The good broad lands, with right good-will."

A smile was in young Nivard's eye,
  While his quick colour went and came;
"These are no equal terms, Sir Guy,"
  He said; "O tell it not for shame,
That this your love's award should be,
Heaven for yourselves, and earth for me."

'Twas past: the wondering band went on,
    And talk'd of Nivard's jesting prate;
But when a few short years were flown,
    There stood before the convent-gate
A grey-hair'd knight, and stripling tall;
"We come," they said; "now Heaven take all!"

L'Envoy.

Those still Cistercian walls are gone;
    And Faith in bondage must abide,
Where tyrants, to her God unknown,
    Rear high their pyramids of pride,
And their hard tasksmen scarce will spare
    The Sabbath-hours for rest and prayer;

And flatterers praise their deeds, and scorn
    Those unenquiring days of old,
Ere stirring Sciences were born,
    And Wealth increased, and Love grew cold!
And teach, for Duty's ancient way,
That to enjoy is to obey.

But thou, fair child, beware their lure,
    That would with notes of peace destroy,
Tempting meek hearts from shades secure
    To griefs that feign the sense of joy;
And rather seek, ere storms be nigh,
The threshold of glad Poverty.

Nor scorn the truth that breathes within
    Those mouldering aisles of Faith o'erthrown,
That souls who mourn for mortal sin
    Must dwell in silence and alone;
That Heaven shines down with purer ray
On virgin souls that watch and pray.

Thou know'st not, how minds innocent,
    In this world's crowded solitude,
With pangs of secret grief are rent,
    And fain would fly to deserts rude,
Where the lone dove may pour her moan
From dewy cave and mossy stone.

Thou know'st not, how that lordship proud,
    That racks the vain with envy's thorn,
With weight of cureless cares is bow'd,
    And they, who have such fardel borne,
More blithe in prison-bands would lie,
Than bide that heart's captivity.

I bid thee not with hood or veil
    To cloud thy sunbright youth in gloom,
But make, ere life's first promise fail,
    Thy Father's house thy freedom's home;
Arms, such as Templar never wore,
Shall meet thee on the Church's floor.

And, with that armour girded on,
    Go forth, and try what Truth can do,
Though singly match'd, yet not alone,
    In combat with a world untrue :
With sweeter rest shalt thou be paid,
Than the glad hart's in noontide shade.

VIII.

WALTER ESPEC.

WALTER ESPEC was a Norman Baron, who possessed large estates in Yorkshire in the reigns of Henry I. and Stephen. His sister Adeline, wife of Peter Lord Roos, was ancestress of the noble house of Manners. He is famous in English history, as the captain to whose courage and conduct the victory of the Standard was mainly owing, and also as the founder of Kirkham and Rievaulx Abbeys; acts of piety to which he was led by parental grief for the loss of an only son, who was killed by a fall from his horse. The authorities for these particulars, and other facts mentioned in the following ballad, are the Latin History of the Battle of the Standard, by Aylred of Rievaulx, and Dugdale's Monasticon, in the account of the above-mentioned Abbeys.

> THE Barons of our island,*
> The princes of the free,
> By lowland or by highland
> Bright may their memory be!

---

* It has been the fashion with too many modern writers to call in question the virtues of the old champions of our native soil, who defended the frontier against Scotland and France, rescued the Christian states in the East, and secured the great Charter of

O, noble was their bearing,
Free Virtue's inborn mood,
Majestic Nature's rearing
In her feudal solitude ;

---

the subject's liberties. "If any sparks of liberty were struck out," says the conceited Horace Walpole, "it was not owing to the separate virtue of flint or steel, but to their collision." Good, from the advocate who came forward to defend the injured virtues of Richard III. "We know," says Mr. Hallam, that a nobility is always insolent." "The Great Charter," says Bishop Warburton, "was wrested from the Crown by a factious, turbulent, and ambitious Baronage, into whose hearts the love of the people never entered."

This is a severe sentence. We have a striking character of one of the Barons who opposed King John, drawn by one who knew him, in the account which Gyraldus Cambrensis has left us of William de Bruce, a Baron whose seat was at the Castle of Brecon, where its ruins are still visible. "Nothing human is perfect," says Gyraldus, "and to know everything, and offend in nothing, is rather the attribute of God than of man. But I think it worthy of mention, that in his ordinary discourse it was this nobleman's custom to set the Lord always before him, saying of everything he took in hand, Let it be done in God's name, or for God's sake ; or if God will ; or By God's grace it shall be so ; following in this the practice of St. Paul, and the precept of St. James. (Acts xviii. 21 ; 1 Cor. iv. 19 ; James iv. 15.) To the scribes who wrote his letters,—and being rich and powerful, he had a large correspondence with many quarters,—he gave a small gratuity in addition to their pay, on condition that they should never forget to begin with a mention of the Divine Mercy, and end with a word of the Divine Aid. When he was on a journey, and came within sight of a church or a cross by the wayside,

> Before the stock was blighted
>   By Mammon's withering ban,
> And blushing Honour knighted
>   The burgher-gentleman.
>
> How well they kept their courses,
>   When in glittering armour bright,
> They wheel'd their gallant horses
>   In the tourney's mimic fight:

---

though he might at the time be engaged in conversation with a companion, whether high or low, he immediately betook himself to his prayers, which being shortly completed, he returned, as from a digression, to the subject of their discourse. What was further remarkable, whenever he met with children on his way, he would invite them with a few kind words to hold a little talk with him, that he might force the little innocents to give him their blessing, and pay it back with his own blessing in return." This does not appear like the character of a man into whose heart the love of his own kind never entered. Other instances might easily be found.

  It is confessed that there was in those warlike times great temptation to the abuse of power, and greater space for the exercise both of conspicuous crimes and great virtues. Let a true knowledge of history teach us, while we abhor the one, to admire and venerate the other; and not condemn them in the mass, because our corrupt age has been pleased to dwell more on the evil than the good. This is my meaning, gentle reader, when I try to remind you that there were virtues in these old Peers of England, which no true lover of his country can forget, and which all who love virtue will seek to imitate.

How courteous were their speeches,
    Meet for gentle lady's ear,
Such as Flattery never teaches;
    They are born in souls sincere.

How oft with eye that glisten'd
    They read the storied page,
Or with bending ears they listen'd,
    When the minstrel, white with age,

Told his tale of days departed,
    And with pity tuned the string
For the chief who died true-hearted,—
    Died for Holy Kirk and King.

For not to pastime solely
    Their hours of peace they gave;
High thoughts and counsels holy
    Attend the good and brave.

And when Religion call'd them,
    Or their country gave the word,
No peril then appall'd them,
    When they drew the rightful sword.

It was no drug that drenches*
    The sense in harm and loss,
That arm'd in Salem's trenches
    The champions of the Cross;

---

* That is, they did not fight under the influence of opium, gentle reader, nor for opium. The Turks, they say, do the first; if you

That arm'd each noble martyr,
    Who died in Freedom's cause,
Ere they won the sacred Charter
    Of England's rescued laws.

Let not Envy's voice upbraid them,
    Now the lion-hearts are gone;
Let them rest where Honour laid them,
    When their valour's task was done;

Where their forms by Sculpture moulded,
    Lie in battle-mail array'd,
And their steel-clad hands are folded
    As though still in death they pray'd;

To tell each gazing stranger,
    That in life's uneven road
The loyal walk with danger,
    And in sleep must wake to God.

Such life was Baron Walter's,
    That chief of old renown,
Lord of the woods of Galtres
    And Cleveland's mountains brown.

---

have ever heard of a nation that has done the second, and that not long ago, why then, perhaps, times are not so very much mended since the Barons' wars. But I hope neither you nor I had any vote in the matter.

One day he had of glory,
    One day to memory dear,
That long in England's story
    The listening world shall hear :

When he stood midst dead and dying,
    On Allerton's broad plain,
Where the bolts from arblasts flying,*
    Drank the blood of Scotland's slain ;

When with eye that never wander'd,
    And with heart that could not yield,
Fast by the noble Standard †
    He kept the stubborn field ;

---

* It seems that the word "arblast" is not in Johnson's or other common dictionaries. It was familiar in old English, and means, as the learned know, a cross-bow. Hence the surname "Arblaster" (*arbalester*, in Speed's Chronicle), which was as easily understood in former days as Archer or Bowman ; but since the Crossbowman was forgotten, has been ridiculously corrupted into Alabaster ; even a poet, Dr. W. Alabaster, in Charles I.'s days, following the common misnomer. One example shall be given from the fine moral verses of old Lydgate :—

    "God hath a thousande handes, if He chastyse,
      A thousande dartes of strange punicion,
      A thousande bowes all made in divers wyse,
      A thousande *arblasts* bent in Hys dongeon ;
      But where He findes mekeness and penitaunce,
    Mercy is mistresse of His ordinaunce."
                    Tragedies of Princes, I. § 3.

† The Standard, which has given name to this famous battle, was

> And his voice amidst the battle
> Was heard at every stound
> Above the din and rattle,
> Like the trumpet's silver sound.

a tall ship-mast set on a four-wheeled carriage; and from it were displayed the three sacred banners of Yorkshire,—that of St. Peter of York, St. Wilfrid of Ripon, and St. John of Beverley. Geoffrey de Vinesauf describes the royal banner of Cœur de Lion, as displayed from a precisely similar Standard in his wars in Palestine. In the south of England there were also sometimes three banners carried, that of St. George, that of St. Edmund, and St. Edward the Confessor. It is singular that of all these, St. George's, a saint whose honour was imported by the Crusaders from the East, should have outlasted the rest, and especially those of four native saints.

Walter Espec, says the historian of Rievaulx, was "a man of stature passing tall, but of limbs well proportioned, and which were well fitted to his great height. He had his hair still black, though he was old and full of days; his beard was long and flowing, his forehead wide and noble, his eyes large and piercing, his face broad but well-featured, and his voice like the sound of a trumpet, setting off his natural eloquence of his speech with a kind of majesty of sound." When he had harangued the army before the battle, and encouraged them not to fear the greater numbers of the Scots, he took the right hand of the Earl of Albemarle, who commanded the English army, and said, "I swear on this day to conquer or die upon the field." "So swear we all," said the other barons; and the fight began. Baron Walter retired from the world, and became a monk at Rievaulx about two years before his death; he died there, March 9, 1153.

But tell me why that old man
    Endured that summer's day,
When many a young and bold man
    Was fain to quit the fray?

What strong resolve had bound him
    To conquer or to die,
While each hardy knight around him
    Caught a courage from his eye?

That ancient Baron Walter,
    His earthly hope was gone,
When he rear'd the solemn altar
    Beneath the vault of stone.

Where the silver Derwent wanders
    By woods and meadows green,
Where the pitying Muse still ponders
    On the things that once have been;

He had rear'd the solemn altar
    Beneath the vault of stone,
Resign'd, though his voice might falter,
    For he mourn'd for his only son.

To God those fruits of sorrow
    His thankful heart had given;
And he rose upon that morrow
    Strong in the strength of heaven.

A courage more than mortal's
    That day had nerved his hand:
"Angels from heaven's high portals
    Would guard his native land;

"Heaven's vengeance should be wroken
    For the blood of infants slain,
And the spoilers' spear be broken,
    And their bodies press the plain."

'Twas done: ere curfew sounded,
    The battle-field was red,
And the northern host, confounded,
    Left twice five thousand dead.

But by the noble Standard,
    When died the battle's roar,
That eye that never wander'd
    Was seen to watch no more.

Where the Rie its waves of amber
    Rolls o'er its bed of stone,
Where the wild deer stray, or clamber
    The grey rocks all alone,

There an abbey stands,—more fair one
    No northern vale hath seen;
That abbey rear'd the Baron
    Those echoing hills between.

There dwell the monks, the wan ones,
    Who labour, fast, and pray,
Good Bernard's meek companions
    In their cowls and frocks of grey.

While the moon is on the mountains,
    And the moonlit air is still;
No sound, save of the fountains,
    Or the gushing near the mill;

Now the midnight chaunt is ended,
    And the aisles are deep in shade,
And in chambers long-extended
    The convent's sons are laid;

Gaze softly, where the grating
    Gives to view the bed of heath,
There the Baron rests, awaiting
    The welcome call of death.

IX.

MARGARET BISSET.

MARGARET BISSET was one of the maids of honour who waited on Eleanor of Provence, queen consort of Henry III. The incident on which the following lines are founded is recorded by Matt. Paris, as having occurred in the autumn of A.D. 1238.

BROAD was the forest's ancient space,*
When England's kings on Woodstock chace,
Oft wearied many a gallant horse,
Hunting the fearful hart of force,†
With cry of hounds, and blasts between,
That woke the jocund woodland scene.

---

* The royal chace at Woodstock, including Whichwood and four adjoining townships, is described in Domesday Book as being nine leagues, or nearly thirty miles, square. The park of Woodstock was enclosed by Henry I., who also built a royal mansion there; but the place had been an ancient seat of the Saxon kings.

† From Lord Surrey's old poem upon Windsor:
"The wylde forest, the clothed holtes with grene,
Where we did chase the fearful hart of force
With crye of houndes and merry blastes betwene."

Returning slow at evening hour,
King Henry sought fair Woodstock's bower,
Alighting at the accustom'd gate,
Where oft, retired from toils of state,
He shared with comrades choice and few
Such mirth as merry England knew.

Strange sight! Emerging from the wood
There came in fierce distracted mood
An outlaw'd knight. With darksome frown
He cried, "False king, resign thy crown:
Restore my rights, usurp'd too long;
Or Heaven, that sees, shall judge the wrong."

The loyal yeomen rear'd their staves,
And marvell'd much, what king of knaves
Was he, who dared to rail so high
In ears of England's Majesty;
But the good king their anger stay'd,
"Let go the poor distraught," he said.

Forgotten was that madman's freak:
It was a merry jest to speak
Of what had chanced, when at the door
His youthful queen, fair Eleanor,
Came down, her lord's return to grace,
And hear each passage of the chace.

But then the jocund feast was spread;
And when the weary guests were fed,
The gleemen came with harp and song,
And other tales the time prolong;
Till lord and lady, host and guest,
Are gone to quiet bed of rest.

One lonely lamp at midnight hour
Stream'd from the gateway's lofty tower,
What time beneath the pale moon's ray
So still the forest mazes lay,
That scarce a breath of roving air
Gave Night a voice to murmur there.

But where that lonely lamp was bright,
A maiden fair kept watch by night,
A maiden gentle, fair, and young,
Who sweetly sang her compline-song,
Before her, on a polish'd stand,
Her psalter-book, her harp in hand.

She was a Baron's daughter, one
Whom proudest fortune smiled upon,
And none of lovelier face or mien
Waited on England's youthful queen:
But suitors vainly came to move
A heart that own'd a higher love.

Oft, when the feast was ranged in hall,
She sought the way-side hospital,
Left the gay masque where dancers meet,
To wash the way-worn pilgrim's feet,
Or watch'd, when life's last hour was nigh,
By age's bed, to learn to die.*

O sight, that angels from the skies
May gaze on with rejoicing eyes,
When gentle youth and beauty bright,
Dead to the vain world's false delight,
Live but to thoughts that saints may share,
And wake by night to songs of prayer!

Her chaunt's last tones had died away:
One moment by the pale moon's ray
She look'd upon the peaceful scene,
And on the bright heaven's deep serene,
Ere yet her couch of needful rest,
At peace, with dreams of peace, she press'd.

---

* These were the charitable works of good ladies in the Middle Ages, as we read of Matilda, queen of Henry I., of Aletta, mother of St. Bernard, and of Margaret, Countess of Richmond. An old author says of Aletta, "She was often to be seen, alone and on foot, on the road between Fontaines and Dijon, visiting the cottages of the poor, and carrying provisions and remedies to the sick and afflicted, and administering instruction and spiritual consolation to them. She never allowed her domestics to assist her in these offices, so that it might truly be said her left hand knew not what her right hand performed."

What turns her startled ear to mark?
Was it the watch-dog's honest bark?
Or wandering night-bird's fitful cry,
That rose afar complainingly?
Again? it is a thought of fear;
A step is in the chamber near.

That chamber where the king full late
Had strewn his regal couch of state,
Till Eleanor had used her power
To change it for a brighter bower,
A brighter bower, more deftly made,
Where now the royal pair were laid.

Fair Margaret down the stair of stone
To that void chamber hastes alone,
With lamp in hand. She turns the key,
And now her eyes a sight may see,
That might a stronger frame o'erpower,
Unused to face sharp danger's hour.

There dimly in the lamp's faint light
Stood forth the maniac outlaw'd knight,
With rugged brow and darting eye;
And to her straight approaching nigh,
Arm'd with a naked glittering blade,
He brandish'd high his hand, and said:

"The false king's fatal hour is come:
Your gate was barr'd; the wall I clomb;
Stole through the window; sought his bed;
Where is the cowering craven fled?
Aid me, I'll swear by yon round moon
To take thee for my queen alone."

There is a power that can subdue
All terror, when the heart is true;
There is a wit that springs to aid
The weakest, where wild threats invade,
O'ermastering Frenzy by the eye
Of calm, undaunted Constancy.

Thus spoke the pure and gentle maid:
"What? shall it then be sung or said
That he who England's crown doth claim,
Forgetful of his knighthood's name,
Like a base thief at midnight crept
To stab his rival while he slept?

"Not such the good defiance brave
That Ryence once to Arthur gave.*

---

* King Ryence of North Wales, whose robe of state was bordered with the beards of eleven subject kings, sent to King Arthur to demand his for the twelfth: but it is supposed that King Arthur proved himself the more cunning shaver of the two. The challenge may be seen in the ballad printed in Percy's Reliques.

No! let us seek the guarded hall,
And wake the slumbering seneschal,
And sound our challenge bold and free:
Sheathe then thy sword, and follow me."

He heard, and changed as with a charm,
Dropp'd at the word his sinewy arm:
The maiden to the guard-room led,
And, while the warders gazed in dread,
Spoke briefly in their captain's ear,
" Sir Giles, ye watch but slackly here."

When next with ruddy morning glow'd
The hawthorn banks of Evenlode,
What praise was heard from every tongue
Of that brave maiden, fair and young,
Who stay'd the wild assassin's knife,
And saved a monarch's sacred life!

Swift roll the winged years away:
Five times hath autumn's misty ray
Lit up on tree and russet heath
The hues that speak of change and death:
In Woodstock gleam the tapers fair
At eve; but Margaret is not there.

Enclosed within the forest wide,
Low roofs and gardens by its side,

A little silvan chapel stood,
Built for a pious sisterhood;
And she whose wealth their vows had blest,
There in the lowly aisle hath rest.*

---

* The lady, whose presence of mind was the means of rescuing her sovereign from this great danger, died at an early age about four years afterwards, when she had founded a nunnery in the neighbourhood, the precise situation of which is not mentioned by the historian. Matt. Paris, in A.D. 1242.

X.

THE BOY OF NAVARRE.

THE fact upon which the following lines are founded occurred at a time when the factions of the English nobles were beginning to be very ruinous to the ancient spirit of chivalry, and dangerous to the public safety, during the early years and minority of Richard II., about A.D. 1377-1380. It is briefly recorded in Walsingham's Chronicle, p. 229, ed. Camd.

A DARK-HAIR'D boy from old Navarre,—
   The gladness of his eye
Glanced radiant, as the silver star
   At gloaming lights the sky.

A page of lighter step, I ween,
   Ne'er tripp'd in lady's bower;
But now with solemn pace and mien,
   In London's frowning Tower,

'Twas his to tend a captive knight,
   Who, fast in cell of stone,
Must bid farewell to all delight,
   Until his cause be known.

The lords are met at council-board;
    With speeches fierce and high,
The rivals of their state, abhorr'd,
    They doom to pine and die.

And now a herald forth is gone,
    Their stern award to bear,
Where worth and valour make their moan
    On prison-bed of care:

"Sir Knight," he said, "in dungeon-hold
    Thy forfeit life must pine,
Till surety mend the strife, and gold
    Assoil thee of thy fine:

"Such grace is offer'd, since thy lance
    Was stout in old Navarre,
And firm in field of fertile France,
    When Edward led the war.

"Three thousand marks the scale may turn,
    And set the prisoner free."
Sir Hubert felt his proud heart burn:
    But then his glance might see

The gentle boy from old Navarre
    Stand smiling silently,
And radiant as a silver star
    The gladness of his eye.

Sir Hubert paused,—perchance for ruth,
    Lest words that spoke annoy
Might seem to wrong his page's truth,
    And dash his childish joy.

The herald parts; and night is come:
    But, ere the morning grey
Shed latticed light within the room,
    The page was on his way;

And where the nobles of the land
    To council-board repair,
He prays their grace with cap in hand,
    The earliest suitor there:

"Barons," he said, "this trusty word
    Sir Hubert sends by me:
A soldier's wealth is his good sword,
    Not land or golden fee;

"But since in Spain he bore him well
    By princely Edward's side,
To him a noble hostage fell,
    Rescued in battle-tide,

"Young Raymond, Count of Deva's son:
    Let him your surety be;
A princely ransom is your own,
    But set Sir Hubert free."

"And where is now Count Raymond's son?"
    Fierce Mowbray quick replied:
The boy drew back; a nobler air
    Spoke from his brow of pride:

"Ere this he were in old Navarre,
    And glad both sire and son,
Had he who saved him in the war
    His gallant purpose done.

"But since upon his patron's fate
    Mischance hath seem'd to lower,
'Tis his to tend his bonds, and wait
    His errand in the Tower."

Then might you see strange passions move
    Those stern-faced lords, each one;
And foremost each to ask they strove,
    "Art thou Count Raymond's son?"

The boy drew off a Spanish glove,
    And show'd a ruby ring:
"A token this my faith to prove,
    I wear it from my king."

Then rose the mitred Sudbury,
    And spoke: "My noble peers,
See heaven reveal truth's mystery
    To childhood's simple years!

" But lest this gipsy boy of Spain
    Should boast our worth outdone,
Free pardon let Sir Hubert gain,
    Speed home Count Raymond's son."

Then back the boy of old Navarre
    To London's Tower might hie,
And brighter than a silver star
    The gladness of his eye.

XI.

THE BATTLE OF VARNA.

THE battle of Varna was fought on November 10, 1444; and was a fatal battle to those Christian states in the East of Europe, which had allied themselves to check the arms of the Turks, and to save Constantinople. The Hungarians and other allies had unhappily listened to the advice of the Pope's Nuncio, who persuaded them to break a ten years' treaty, just concluded on very advantageous terms to themselves, with the Turkish Sultan. Hence Christian writers have always spoken of this overthrow as a token of God's judgment against the truce-breakers; and the contemporary authorities mention the anecdote of Amurath, which is here related, in reference to it.

THRICE, like crested seas advancing,
    Where tall rocks their inroad bar,
On the strong Hungarian border
    Roll'd the Moslem waves of war:
Thrice that broken surge retreating
    Left its corpses strew'd in gore,
Like the green and purple tangles
    By the wave-mark on the shore.

Then said Amurath the Sultan,
 "Allah, thou art great alone!
Fatal is this cloud that gathers
 Round the Balkan's mountain-throne.
By the faithful fall'n around me
 Well I read the sure decree:
Fate ordains a further conquest,—
 But to mine, and not to me.
Brave viziers, now let the sabre
 Spare the foes whom we abhor,
Till the star of young Mohammed
 Lights anew the ranks of war;
Let soft peace restore the weary,
 Till Mohammed's beard be grown,
And his sword shall lead to glories
 I too rashly deem'd my own."

Straight a herald sped the message,
 That the wide-encroaching Turk,
Yielding now his claim of conquest,
 Sought a truce from murder's work.
Soon they met,—the Reis Effendi
 With his sable-silver'd beard,
And Hunniades the Waiwode,
 Whom the turban'd Othmans fear'd:
Glad Hungaria's war-worn monarch
 Gave the truce the Moslems pray'd;
Glad his warriors saw returning
 Sabbath-rest with God to aid.

Fair and free the term accorded,
    Till ten times the circling sun
O'er the wide Hungarian border
    His full yearly course had run.
But, alack the day! Pope Eugene,
    Frowning from his solemn throne,
Proudly spoke, "This peace ill-sorted
    Mars the good that valour won.
Christian knights, too soon ye yielded,
    And by evil arts o'erseen;
Let this poor and bootless treaty
    Be as it had never been."
Such the message Juliano
    From the Roman father bore:
"Keep no truce with unbelievers;
    Void are all the oaths ye swore."
Bold the Cardinal and Legate
    Stand before the Christian peers;
Arm'd he comes to lead the battle,
    High the banner'd Cross he rears.
But, alack! that day of sorrow,
    When the champions of the Cross
Listen'd to his faithless message,
    Spring of fatal harm and loss.

Strong in arms the Christian squadrons
    Left the pine-clad mountain-brow,
And the sword's wide-wasting onset
    Swept Bulgaria's plains below;

Still the Moslem host retreated,
    Till, in Varna's spreading bay,
They beheld where now the Sultan
    With his fleet at anchor lay:
"Onward!" cried Hungaria's monarch,
    "Till our mountain eagle lave
Her bold breast and gory pinions
    In dark Euxine's stormy wave.
Onward! till the recreant Paynim
    From our Christian land retire;
Or the sea engulph the remnant
    'Scaped from battering sword and fire."

Then the shout of gathering thousands
    Echoed to the trumpet's breath,
Scorn was there, and maddening laughter,
    And the baneful joys of death:
Onward rush'd Hungaria's monarch,
    Loud he raised his battle-cry,
As he near'd the stern-eyed Sultan:
    "Amurath, now fight or fly."
From his breast the stern-eyed Sultan
    Drew a scroll of parchment fair:
Briefly to and fro he waved it
    In the clear and sunbright air:
"Jesu, son of maiden Mary,
    Whom the Christian hosts adore,
Carest Thou not for these deceivers,
    Who Thy name blaspheming swore?

Lo! the scroll of truce! the signet!
   'Tis their king's imperial sign:
Be it Thine to chasten falsehood,
   If to preach of truth were Thine."

Was it that the Lord of Glory
   Heard the Paynim chieftain's prayer,
Or that heaviest vengeance ever
   Waits on Christians who forswear?
Straight, as when some counter-current
   Rolls the eddying clouds away,
Back the tide of war returning
   Changed the fortune of that day.
Low then fell Hungaria's monarch,
   Low was Julian's pride o'erthrown,
Brave Hunniades borne backward
   Lives to lose his rescued throne.
From that day in prouder conquest
   Did the wavering Crescent shine,
Till it storm'd thy princely bulwarks,
   Brave and peerless Constantine!

XII.

STRAFFORD.

THE Defence of Lord Strafford, spoken on April 12, 1641, was published among the pamphlets of the day. It appears to have been taken down by a reporter, who had heard it delivered, and was able to give the substance of the concluding portion; but from some errors in the phraseology and arrangement of the sentences, it is evident that we have not the exact words which he used, nor a copy of them revised by himself. We have, therefore, nothing more than a tolerable newspaper report of that Defence, which moved the wondering admiration of all who heard it; and it is important to notice this, as some modern historians have treated it as a document of higher authority. It is from this pamphlet, printed in 1641, that the first part of the following lines has been derived. The rest is partly from the common histories, partly from Sir George Radcliffe's Memoir.

Persons judge differently of the character of Lord Strafford, according to their persuasion of the political condition of England at that time. Those who think that the opponents of this great man had no object but to secure the subject's liberties, and the rights of the House of Commons, and the redress of some acknowledged disorders in the system of government, can only regard this nobleman as a splendid culprit whose fall was just and necessary. Those who, on the contrary, take the view, which the result goes far enough to justify, that there was a powerful faction at work from the first, whose design was to subvert the throne and exalt themselves upon its ruins, must ever revere his character, as an example of fortitude and self-devoted loyalty, such as has never been surpassed.

It is needless to say which of these two opinions the present writer considers to be most in accordance with historical truth. Not even those, who are most strongly under the power of the opposite opinion, will now justify the mode by which this noble victim was sacrificed, doomed to death by a law made for the special purpose of his destruction; but one of the most able advocates who have lately appeared on that side, the ingenious Mr. Hallam, borrowing the words of a second-rate pagan poet, says that, in the case of such conspicuous guilt, some enormity of punishment is requisite, to "absolve the gods," to show that heaven is neither deaf nor blind. A mode of argument which would go to justify, as, indeed, it was first used to justify, an act of public assassination.

Silent were England's peers,
    When Strafford's voice was heard;
A soul too great for the storms of fate
    Spoke in each burning word:

"Such lot," he said, "is mine,
    As the fisher's, doom'd to go,
Where no buoy afloat warn'd his light-oar'd boat
    Of the anchor moor'd below:

"Or like to his, who treads
    The treacherous battle-plain,
Where never smoke from the deep earth broke,
    To mark war's hidden train.

"Let your oracles of law
    Declare, nor think it scorn,
When hath traitor bled on treason's bed
    For a treason yet unborn?

"And ye, high England's peers,
    Shall they say in after time,
That ye gave to hate the power of fate,
    To change the marks of crime?

"Pause yet, if any care
    For your King's just honour be;
Faith will not live, where she may not give
    The counsel of the free.

"O, born to counsel thrones,
  Guard well from harm secure,
From envious breath, and the fear of death,
  That birthright high and pure:

"And give these curious arts,
  That would slay before they warn,
Such end as took old Sorcery's book *
  In Truth's immortal morn.

"Think not, for brittle life
  This constant soul shall sue:
But I plead the cause of England's laws,
  For England, and for you.

"Yet something my heart would say,—
  Those pledges, whom Mercy gave,
Whom a saint at rest, where the pure are blest,
  Still loves beyond the grave,—

---

* See Acts xix. 19. There was a peculiar propriety in Lord Strafford's comparison of the mysterious science of constructive treason, by which he was condemned, with the "curious arts" of the old pagan sorcerers. Both these arts and sciences gave the adepts some especial facilities in practising against human life. And as we read of wizards and fortune-tellers being much patronised by such persons as the Emperor Tiberius and Louis XI. of France, Cromwell also had his Sidrophel in William Lily, who was his astrologer in state affairs.

Must they too share the loss
My heavy doom shall bring?
Nay, the thought was wrong; let my hope be strong
In God, and my gracious King:

"In God, Whose grace hath taught
My weakness to despise
Fate's darkest frown, for the weightier crown
Of glory in the skies.

"And thus, for death or life
Howe'er your voice be given,
There is One alone Whose Will is done,
In this low earth, and heaven."

Silent were England's peers:
The man they would condemn
So calm appear'd, as though he fear'd
Less for himself than them;

And they, who had met to doom
That noble Earl to die,
Shrunk, pale as death, and with bated breath,
From his lion port and eye.

None acted such a part
Upon Fate's purple stage:
O wondrous power of that strong hour,
When Reason strove with Rage!

But the grim award is past;
They have heard him plead in vain :
God pity their toil in the serpent coil
Of Error's endless train !*

And a white-stoled man is gone †
The fatal scroll to bring,
And with fatal art to play his part,
To palter with his King.

O grief ! the King bends down
To write the deathful sign !
" Brave Earl, thy fate, o'erborne by hate,
Is happier far than mine." ‡

O bitter hour of shame,
When, weak to hold his own,
The sad King gave his champion brave
To the foes that sought his throne !

---

* This line, from Spenser's Fairy Queen, I. i. 18, was applied by Strafford himself to the weak or treacherous conduct of other members of the government, by whom his fall was either hastened or contrived. Letter to S. G. Radcliffe, Nov. 5, 1640.

† Williams, Archbishop of York, who told the king he had two consciences, a private and public one; and that he ought only to consult the public one on matters of state.

‡ Charles spoke these words with tears, when he signed the commission to pass the bill. Sir G. Radcliffe's Memoir.

O heaviest wrong to bear
In all that tide of ill!
But a willing mind no wrong can find,*
And Strafford is loyal still.

The pleasant morn of May
Glanced bright on field and bower,
When the solemn bell for that noble knell
Rang out from the frowning Tower.

He comes, that champion brave,
As firm in step and mien,
As in youth he play'd, where the dun deer stray'd
In Wentworth forest green.

He comes, where the rebel rout
Are flocking fast, to see
How the souls of the brave can pass to the grave
In the hour of their agony.

Yet, hold a little space,
And list to the solemn prayer
From the latticed cell, where a priest doth dwell,†
Like him, a captive there;

---

* "To a willing man no injury is done." Strafford's words to the King from the Tower, May 4, 1641.

† For these lines on the parting interview between Strafford and Laud, the writer is much indebted to a friend who sent him his thoughts in manuscript.

A reverend aged priest,
  Who maketh prayer alway;
Though his robes of pride be cast aside,
  And his mitre reft away:

God's chosen priest and true,
  By the rabble's curse o'erborne,
Reserved to feel grim Faction's steel,
  And glut the rebel's scorn.

Before him Strafford kneels:
The knee that could not bow
To crested pride * on Oppression's side.—
It kisses the pavement now;

And up to that aged man
  He meekly lifts his eye,
And in reverent fear he waits to hear
  His blessing, ere he die.

O, those lips for grief are mute:
  He may not speak, but sigh;
And he raiseth his hands in their iron bands,
  And blesseth him silently.

---

* "He loved justice for justice itself, taking great delight to free a poor man from a powerful oppressor, or to punish bold wickedness. This lost him some men's good will, which he thought to be better lost than kept on such terms." Sir G. Radcliffe.

'Tis past :—lead quickly on ;
Deep silence let there be,
Till the words are said, and the prayer is pray'd,
And the gallant soul is free !

XIII.

SAMPSON HORTON.

In the parish Register of Bishop's Bourne, in Kent, is to be seen the following record :—" Sampson Horton was buried the 9th of May 1648; an aged man who had been clarke to this parish, by his own relation, threescore years." He is, therefore, the "grateful clerk," who honoured the memory of Hooker in the way which will be remembered by most readers of Izaak Walton, and which is the subject of the following lines. The anecdote has lately called forth some beautiful verses from a young American divine and poet, the Rev. Benj. Winslow; which the present writer would have preferred inserting in this volume to his own, had it not appeared that they were not sufficiently cast into the narrative form required in a ballad.

> The drops of kindly dew * that fall
> From trees of goodliest bough,
> Rain blessings on each flow'ret small,
> That lowly blooms below.

---

* Spenser, Shepherd's Calendar, November :—
  " The kindly dewe drops from the higher tree,
  And wets the little plants that lowly dwell."

Such grace have souls of highest grace,
    By heav'n-taught wisdom made
The strength of men in humbler place,
    Who grow beneath their shade.

Such grace had he, whom Meekness bore
    Most near with Truth to dwell,
With deepest draughts of holy lore
    Fed from the eternal Well,—

The meek-eyed priest of Bishop's Bourne,
    Whom England's Church alway
Deems brightest star that rose at morn
    To light her purer day.

Such grace had he,—and of his grace
    A simple soul had share,
An honest heart, that kept its place
    Amidst a realm's despair,
Nor change nor peril could efface
    The master's lesson there.

Full forty years had come and fled,
    Since that meek man of God
Had lowly laid his reverend head
    Beneath the churchyard sod:

And now new people fill the land,
    To his good name unknown;
New priests at England's altars stand,
    New kings usurp her throne.

Old Sampson Horton, still he lives,
    Hath every change out-worn;
With age to do his part he strives
    Lay-clerk of Bishop's Bourne.

Oft when around the mountain's brow
    The storm beats loud and shrill,
Deep in the winding vale below
    The charmed air is still:

So fared this humble man,—his life
    In Kent's low vales was led;
The thunder of the public strife
    Roll'd high above his head.

Till on a day,—unblest the day,—
    Rebellion's hateful scorn
Forced from his pastoral home away
    The loyal priest of Bourne.

Glad Easter morn was shining bright:
    Old Sampson, as of yore,
With staff to prop his feeble might,
    Took forth his sacred store,

And paten, cup, and linen white,
    For God's blest altar bore.

But where was now glad Easter's song,
    Or Easter's solemn prayer?
Strange features in the chancel throng,
    Strange hands the feast prepare.

And now the graceless rites begin,
    Where men of pride and gloom
Are bold to act fierce Korah's sin,
    And dread not Korah's doom:

With knees that scorn to bow, they meet
    Around the sacred board,
And seats they spread, to sit and eat
    As equals with their Lord.

Awhile old Sampson gazing stood,—
    For age is grave and slow,—
As one scarce able, if he would,
    To comprehend that show.

Then spake Geneva's minister,
    As proud he trod the floor,
"Old man, leave off that wondering air,
    And close the church's door."

"Nay, shut me out," the old man said,
    "My charge I here resign;

Full threescore years that board I spread
    For other rites than thine,
And knelt, where prayer had bless'd the bread,
    Salvation's pledge and sign.

" Not mine the part of questions deep,
    That oft perplex the wise ;
But firm to death that path to keep,
    Where simple duty lies.

" Where my good master bow'd, I bow ;
    Age keeps its memories strong,—
I cannot change my service now,
    I cannot do him wrong."

He left the desecrated dome ;
    A tear was in his eye ;
He sought his humble cottage-home,
    And laid him down to die.

Light lie the earth upon his breast
    Beneath the churchyard sod,
Where Hooker's honour'd bones at rest
    Await the trump of God :

And when for me some tangled knot
    Perplexing Reason ties,
Some Angel guide me to that spot
    Where simple Duty lies !

XIV.

ELISABETH STUART.

In the month of November 1793, as some workmen were digging a grave in the chancel of the church at Newport in the Isle of Wight, they discovered a leaden coffin, on which was inscribed the name and title of "Elisabeth, second daughter of the late King Charles, Sept. 8, 1650." It was then almost a forgotten tale, that this young princess, with her little brother the Duke of Gloucester, after the martyrdom of her royal father, had passed some time under the care of the Earl and Countess of Leicester at Penshurst; but were afterwards removed, by order of the rebel Parliament, to the custody rather than the charge of Sir Henry Mildmay, Governor of Carisbroke Castle, one of the worst men of their own profligate number. Here the tender and delicate girl shortly fell a victim, at the early age of fifteen, to her own acute sorrows; the very place, as her physician said of it, and the remembrance of her father's imprisonment, having raised in her the grief which ended her days. The Duke of Gloucester was afterwards sent by Cromwell's order to join the Queen-Mother in France. He died shortly after the Restoration, in his twentieth year, September 13, 1660, a young prince of the highest promise.

I stood within the mouldering tower,
　　Where once a suffering Monarch lay,
When rebel rage was arm'd with power,
　　And triumph'd in a realm's decay.

The fig-tree wild, that grows on tombs,
　　For sacred sorrow marks the spot;
And there the blue-eyed flowcret blooms,
　　By shepherds call'd Forget-me-not.

That quiet scene,—I know not how,—
　　The roofless walls, the casement's frame,
Where through the bars at freedom now
　　The thymy breezes went and came,—

The turf's green floor within the cell
　　Of that majestic captive's woes,
Moved thoughts too deep for speech to tell,
　　As all the past in memory rose.

Forget thee, martyr'd Saint and King!
　　Forget thee! Sooner let me be
Myself an unremember'd thing
　　To each loved heart that beats for me!

Thus mused I, speaking half aloud,
　　As though that little summer flower
Reproach'd my curious gaze, too proud
　　For mourner in a martyr's bower.

A martyr's bower! Ah, not alone
    For him my vows perform'd shall be;
But for that meek and tender one
    Here doom'd a longer woe to drie;

For her, poor child, whose heavy lot
    It was to bear long months of pain
E'en here, where each remember'd spot
    Recall'd a father's griefs again;

Where, far from every eye that loved,
    Her life's young bloom in charge was given
To one dark soul, as far removed
    From pity, as from hope and heaven.

O witchcraft of rebellious sin,
    That drugs so deep guilt's deadly bowl,
That no sweet Mercy wakes within
    The slumber of the darken'd soul!

O fearful sacraments of crime,
    Which men of blood as pledges seek,
That no remorse in after-time
    May prove them changelings, soft and weak!

Such spell was on thy graceless end,
    Fall'n Mildmay,* of all truth forlorn,
Traitor to all who call'd thee friend,
    At once the rebels' drudge and scorn.

---

* Lord Clarendon gives the following account of this person :

Thy gallant brother,* now to thee
No brother, watch'd his master dear,
And when his gracious soul was free,
To Windsor bore his honour'd bier.

—" He was master of the King's Jewel-house, and had been bred up in the Court, being younger brother of a good family in Essex, and had been prosecuted with so great favours and bounties by King James and by King Charles, that he was raised by them to a great estate and preferred to that office in the Household, which is the best under those which entitle the officers to be of the Privy Council. No man was more obsequious than he to the Court whilst it flourished; a great flatterer of all persons in authority, and a spy in all places for them. But, from the beginning of the Parliament, he concurred with those who were most violent against the Court, and most likely to prevail against it; and being thereupon branded with ingratitude, as that brand commonly makes men impudent, he continued his desperate pace with them, till he became one of the murderers of his master." He and another wretched apostate, Sir John D'Anvers, were the only persons who sat as judges on the Royal Martyr, whom he had personally known. These two had both been his confidential and highly-favoured servants, and consequently we may well believe what Lord Clarendon says, that "the party of miscreants," who profited by their baseness, " looked upon no two men in the kingdom with such scorn and detestation, as they did on D'Anvers and Mildmay."

* Antony Mildmay, Esq., the younger brother of Sir Henry, was the exact opposite to him in all points of his character. Stedfast in his religion, and loyal to his sovereign to the end, he waited on him in prison at Carisbroke, and at Hurst Castle; and attended his corpse with the faithful Sir Thomas Herbert, when it was carried from London to be buried at Windsor.

But thou, who didst consent to bring
    That stately cedar down so low,
Wouldst now too strike the shoots of spring,
    That from its root in beauty grow.

Beneath that withering jailer's eye,
    The child,—so dark his glances were,—
Oft pray'd, if Heaven would bid her die,
    That doom had less of fear for her.

And when in many a rise and fall
    The winds swept round these turrets grey,
She deem'd she heard her father call
    Her suffering soul no more to stay.

For still his voice was in her ear,[*]
    As when, his last farewell to speak,
He raised her faint and mute with fear,
    And kiss'd her pale cold trembling cheek;

---

[*] The Princess Elisabeth, as it is well known, left a short and simple account in writing of her and her brother's last interview with her father before his death; of which a most affecting relation is given by Herbert. Later writers have commonly repeated the account of the words which passed between the little Duke of Gloucester and his father; but have been less particular about those which the Princess relates as addressed to herself, to which allusion is here made:

"He wished me not to grieve and torment myself for him; for that it would be a glorious death that he should die, for the laws and liberties of this land, and for maintaining the true Pro-

And pray'd Heav'n's grace to shield her youth,
  To guard her soul with holiest care,
By Laud and Hooker train'd in truth,
  By Andrewes taught the voice of prayer.

" Grieve not for me," her sire had said,
  " For I shall win the martyr's wreath."
" O no, I grieve not; but my head
  Throbs with an eager pulse for death."

It was the fever of the brain
  That wrought to death that gentle dove ;—
But oh, she hath not lived in vain,
  Young martyr vow'd of filial love.

---

testant religion. He bade me read Bishop Andrews's Sermons, Hooker's Ecclesiastical Polity, and Bishop Laud's Book against Fisher, which would ground me against Popery. He told me he had forgiven his enemies, and hoped God would forgive them ; and commanded us, and all the rest of my brothers and sisters, to forgive them. He bade me tell my mother that his thoughts had never strayed from her, and that his love should be the same to the last. He commanded me and my brother to be obedient to her, and bade me send his blessing to the rest of my brothers and sisters, with commendation to all his friends. So after he had given me his blessing, I took my leave.

" Further, he commanded us all to forgive those people, but never to trust them ; for they had been most false to him, and to those that gave them power, and he feared to their own souls also. He desired me not to grieve for him, for he should die a martyr, and he doubted not but that God would settle his throne upon his son, and that we should be all happier than we could have expected to have been if he had lived."

TWO SONNETS,

MEDITATED IN GRASMERE CHURCHYARD.

I.

WE trod the Vale of peaceful Memory,
    Where He, whose thoughts were hung on every bough,
    Whose spirit linger'd round each mist-clad brow,
Or glanced from every dewy flow'ret's eye,
Was with us; where each breeze that murmur'd by,
    The torrent's roar amidst the silent wood,
    The still dark mirror of the moonlit flood,
Woke in the soul mysterious harmony,
    And joy of voiceless songs; till one green nook
    Subdued us, where one simple dark grey stone
Marks the low mound, where sleeps the minstrel tongue,
Of Him whose harp meek Mercy tuned and strung,
    Whom gentlest Nature for her Prophet took,
    And Love Eternal hallow'd for its own.

II.

Flow on, bright Rotha, sparkling to the day,
    Roll thy clear waves o'er moss or serried stone,
    Whether the mountain storms with flash and moan
Swell thy full stream, or on its summer way
It sport midst birchen shades and marble grey,
    Undimm'd alike and pure. For such was One,
    Who listen'd to thy voice, and caught its tone,
Brightening earth's joys, or chiding grief away
    With flow of song untroubled. Who would change
That life, whose music countercharm'd despair,
    For Wealth's dead surging sea, where never oar
    Or sail yet found the visionary shore,
Or all Ambition's madness? Whisperings strange
Breathe from that grave. Peace sings her requiem
    there!

September 1851.

A VISION OF THE HILLS.

Was it a dream that mock'd my waking sight,
   As stretch'd upon the mountain-slope I lay,
   And wondering saw the deep blue vault of day
Converge as to a hollow spire of light,
Wherein a stair of sapphire, height on height,
   Rose circling still, till eye no more could trace
The lessening rounds, so spiritually bright,
   That angel forms might seem to throng the space
Ascending or descending? Was it vain,
   That show, which all unbidden met my gaze?
   Or was th' unearthly pageant sent to raise
The drooping heart, and bid the soul be strong,
Till loosed from earthly bonds it rise to gain
Heights, where Heaven's choirs attune th' eternal song?

On Skiddaw, Sept. 1, 1854.

THOUGHTS OF ROBERT SOUTHEY,

AT GRETA HALL.

I.

Was ever Poet nursed in school like thine,
   Mid sighs of furnace-blasts, and sobs of mills,
   In tunnel-reek, and steams of spirit-stills,
Where scarce the sun's meridian beams might shine?
Did ever infant Poet pen a line
   By money-changers' boards, or tinkling tills?
   Or learn to lisp in numbers, taught by bills
Of strollers, scorn of Phœbus and the Nine?
Yet Nature made thy joyous heart a mine
   Of fancies rich, as throng the sunbright hills,
   Or wake at morn by Heliconian rills,
As gay as merry Greece, and more benign;
   Warm fancies, proof to stormy Fortune's chills,
That burn at Home-Affection's altar-shrine.

                    1854.

II.

PROUD bards there are, who Fortune's power defy,
    And say she bears no sway where Prudence dwells:
There are, who from her threats dishearten'd fly,
    Whose new-fledged hopes her first rude tempest quells;
Who sing their idle griefs to woods and dells,
Like the poor brainsick knight, in field o'erthrown,
    Of whose last dolorous trance the Spaniard tells,
Vowing to make the shepherd's life his own,
And leave his lance to rust. A braver tone
    Was thine, to smile at Fate that frown'd on thee,
To teach the sullen world how thou hadst won
    The gladness of the heart by Truth set free,
And, more than laureate wreath, the crown made sure
To virtuous aims fast-link'd with counsels pure.

                      1854.

DEDICATORY SONNET

PREFIXED TO THE AUTHOR'S "GONGORA," WITH A GRATEFUL INSCRIPTION "TO THE PIOUS MEMORY OF ROBERT SOUTHEY, THE FRIEND OF SPAIN AND OF SPANISH LITERATURE."

I THOUGHT of thee on stern Sebastian's height,
    Gazing on rock, and flood, and sounding shore,
And sparkling waves that danced in Eastern light,
    While Morn her orange-wreath in beauty wore:
    I heard the broad Atlantic's solemn roar,
Look'd to the stedfast hills, and thought of thee
    Bidding thy bedes at Mercy's golden door,
Till Pride was quell'd, and suffering realms were free;
That evermore the pine-clad Pyrenee
    Might be this loyal Land's unbroken zone,
And Truth, more fair than Morn o'er sparkling sea,
    Might dawn to blend long-sever'd faiths in one.
Shall it not come, that dawn of Truth so fair?
Thy spirit lives, and Heaven records the prayer!

NORTH-COUNTRY RIVERS.

Fair Wharfe, glad pastoral Yore, bright Swale, loud
    Tees,
  Clear sparkling Rother, and dark Lune, your throng
  Of waters rolls as from the Fount of Song,
The living chaunt of heaven's deep harmonies:
Strange spirits haunt your caves, your rocks, your trees,
  Leap down your torrent-falls, or dart along
  Your sunbeams, glancing, changing, swift and strong,
With shafts new-bathed in glory. Let soft Ease,
Sleep by the still broad lake or tranquil shore,
Where rest is pleasant and the land is good:
Let Mammon dig and delve for glittering ore
Amidst the world's dry places, bleak and rude:
But, Hope, thy call speaks from each arrowy flood
The Eternal's watchword, Onward evermore!

        Near Ingleborough, Sept. 28, 1864.

IONA.

THE glittering shafts of Morn
  Are glancing o'er the waves,
And dart from misty hills of Lorn
  On Mull's sea-weltering caves.

Aboard, young hearts, with me !
  We steer by stormy shores,
Where pent in straits the northern Sea
  Round rock and headland roars.

'Tis past, the surging Sound :
  And, righting from the strain,
Our bark, like steed in meadow-ground,
  Is racing through the main.

Care not for weeping cloud,
  Again the sun shall smile,
And hang its rainbow's emerald shroud
  On Staffa's wondrous isle.

Yet not on Staffa's isle
  Our wish shall linger long,
Though well may Nature's vaulted pile
  Wake up our choral song.

We seek a dearer land,
    That boasts a richer store
Than ere from Ophir's golden strand
    Tyre's merchant-princes bore :

There sleep the saintly dead,
    Whom from their island-home
The Baptist's hermit spirit led
    O'er moss and moor to roam.

Where soft as spring-tide dew
    Their gracious speech was heard,
Wild tribes, whom Cæsars never knew,
    Bow'd captive to the Word :

In tempest-girdled Thule
    The Northmen sought their lore,
And blue-eyed Saxons learnt their rule,
    On far Northumbria's shore.

Tread softly o'er the ground :
    The forms we may not see
Perchance e'en now are hovering round
    From earthly trammels free.

Though mute these aisles that rang
    With voice of chaunted prayer,
Or echoing but with sea-bird's clang
    Through arches rude and bare,

The spirit of their love
    Breathes yet from every stone,
Their toil, whose record lives above,
    To mortal praise unknown.

Though cold that love in death,
    And Discord wild and wide,
Strong in the wreck of ancient Faith,
    Walks forth on every side,

Yet let thy vow be said,
    For Truth to do and dare,
The spirits of the saintly dead
    Are near to bless thy prayer:

The sun is bright above
    The sounding northern main,
And bright-eyed Faith shall shine and move
    United hearts again.

August 25, 1857.

KILLIECRANKIE.

Oh for one hour of brave Dundee!
    That last strong hour by Garry's flood,
Which saw his victor-soul set free
    By Death and Fortune unsubdued!

When the mute caves in deepest glen,
    The cliffs with birchen sprays o'erhung,
Rang echoing to the deeds of men
    Unmatch'd since Earth and Time were young;

When Honour, from her beaming throne,
    Smiled on her champion's rugged fight,
Gilding with brightest set of sun
    The last proud field of Scotland's right.

Roll on, swift Garry, down the glen,
    Swift as the rolling war that day,
Led by that peerless Chief of men,
    Unchanged by Time and Faith's decay.

Roll thy dark waves by moss-clad rock,
    Through eddying fall, and whirlpool deep,
As voicing still the battle-shock
    Of him who sleeps the warrior's sleep;

And tell, till dull Oblivion die,
　　How here he closed his loyal strife
In thunder-clangs of victory,
　　To live in song a deathless life.

There are, who school their patient breast
　　To bear the imperious spurns of Crime,
To suffer, and in silence rest
　　Through dim reproach, and faithless time.

I blame them not: may rest be theirs,
　　Who dwell at home with blameless peace,
Whose meek enduring soul outwears
　　Hard days, till guile and wrong shall cease.

But meet it is, that Virtue find
　　Her chosen few, of aims more high,
Whom Force may break, but may not bind,
　　Who dare for truth to do and die.

To die, if Fate her doom have pass'd,
　　Their life, but not their faith, to yield,
And bear in death the word that graced
　　The dying Spartan's dinted shield.

August 29, 1855.

GLENCOE.

I STOOD within the vale of woe,
    And saw tall cliffs, in terror piled,
Dark rifts, where torrents leap and flow,
    Loud moaning through the long-drawn wild:

I stood and gazed on stern Glencoe,
    And thought upon the bitter day,
When Murder dyed the mountain-snow
    With stains that ne'er shall pass away;

When Wrath in Council's solemn place
    Rejected pity's suit unheard,
And loosed upon his fiery chase
    Revenge that waited for the word;

When guiltless blood cried out to heaven;
    And despots cold with marble eye
Withheld the sword, which God had given
    To bid the blood-stain'd felon die;

For hard state-reasons steel'd the heart;
    The doubtful throne,—the shifting time,—
And taught the close usurper's art
    To wink at serviceable crime.

"Fair words make truce," King William said;
   His men of arms brought speeches fair:
For them the board their victims spread,
   Nor deem'd that Joab's sword was there.

Within the hospitable door
   The day went down in mirth and glee;
The morrow dawn'd,—O never more
   May sun so dire a dawning see!

Suspicion slept: no guarded watch
   Forewarned, when fell destruction came,
Till ruthless hands were on the latch,
   To heap the hearth with blood and flame.

But who shall tell the piteous strife,
   When babes and mothers, roused to fly,
Lost on steep rocks their feeble life,
   Or sank in wreaths of snow to die?

"A thousand years that mountain-snow
   May melt in mists of vernal rain,
And bathe the slopes of steep Glencoe,
   And wake its vales to joy again;

"But evermore that stain shall last:"—
   I spoke, and Cona's mournful roar
Made answer through the rock-bound waste,
   "For evermore! for evermore!"

August 27, 1857.

A DIRGE AT CULLODEN.

O MOURN for Scotland's noblest,
   The fearless ones and true,
Who fell on drear Culloden,
   By Moray's waters blue.

Let the tear-drop fall above them,
   Where the soil, for which they bled,
Gave wide its rugged bosom
   To strew their funeral bed :

Where the mounds are thrown, chance-scatter'd,
   O'er the unrecorded brave,
As the toil-worn hands of sorrow
   In haste prepared their grave :

Where Scotland o'er her children
   Would have rear'd the sculptured stone,
But, forlorn and grief-enfeebled,
   Left half her task undone.

For who should write the blazon
   Of the dim and evil day,
When the German bands, twice broken,
   Came in turn to stab and slay?

A DIRGE AT CULLODEN.

When the banner'd cross of England
    Droop'd sad in tainted air;
When the coward's wrath was cruel,*
    And his vengeance could not spare?

Nay, in silence and in sadness
    Leave the grey and lonely heath,
Whence Pity fled, all weeping,
    From the victor's sullied wreath;

Where the blood of priceless valour
    Was pour'd on earth like rain,
And the hearts of doleful mothers
    Died down amidst their slain.

Leave, leave the broken column;
    Let the tomb of trophied stone
Tell of Britain's stainless triumphs,
    Not her carnage of her own.

Yet mourn not for the fallen:
    They have found their bed of rest
In the birth-soil of their fathers,
    With the dead who loved them best:

---

* "He was a coward, and *therefore* merciless."—Sir Walter Raleigh of a character in ancient history. I believe this to be a sentence expressive of an universal truth, and therefore think it a mistake to call William, Duke of Cumberland, a brave man.

Where they rush'd, like mists of morning,
    While the cannon's fiery breath
But served to light them onwards
    To the gleaming ranks of death:

When each hand set firm the bonnet
    On each pale and kindling brow,
And closer drew the tartan
    As they vow'd the warrior's vow,

And grasp'd their fathers' broadswords,
    And bade to hill and sky
Their bold farewell that morrow,
    When they went to do and die.

But mourn for hopes that wither'd
    Never more to bloom again;
Mourn the onward road of glory
    Turn'd to Exile's flight of pain;

Mourn for him, the Heir of Princes,
    Whose brightest day of prime,
Fast-fleeting, left his manhood
    A wreck to Change and Time.

Mourn his life of aims forsaken,
    The homeless wanderer's home,
The mirth of heartless revels,
    Where gladness could not come:

A DIRGE AT CULLODEN.

Through graceless courts, heart-weary,
    Unfriended doom'd to rove,
Where none were near to love him,
    None left whom he might love.

Mourn for Him, whom Honour mourned for,
    And scarce could deem the same,
Who had stood, a kingdom's wonder,
    In the front of steel and flame.

When Memory, self-accusing,
    Had bedimm'd the eye of faith,
And the rest was but the anguish
    Of the spirit's living death.*

Mourn for Him ;—but not for Scotland,
    Who fearless sons and true
Sleep well on drear Culloden,
    By Moray's waters blue.

                      August 27, 1855.

---

* "*De vivre et pas vivre est beaucoup plus que de mourir.*" A sentence found in the handwriting of Charles Edward after his death.

A. G. F. P.

"WHAT is that name that changeth not,
　　Though it be turn'd and turn'd again?"
My God-child ADA's: be her lot
　　A life unchanged by joy or pain.
But what strange things that life shall see,
　　We cannot know, we may not plan:
One prayer her name shall teach to me,
　　That all may end as it began!

October 1849.

NURSERY SONG.

AN INCIDENT FROM THE PERSONAL MEMOIRS OF THE RIVER WISKE.

The River Wiske
It took a frisk
Upon a summer's day,
  And roll'd its flood
  In gamesome mood,
Across the Queen's highway.

  Proud of its luck,
  Each little duck
Came forth to dive and play,
  And wish'd the Wiske
  Would take that frisk
On every summer's day.

  But 'twas great risk
  For Kirby Wiske,
The folks were in dismay:
  "O what a flood!
  It bodes no good!
'Twill drown us if we stay."

With puzzled face
Old Boniface
Peep'd from his door that day,
  For fear his ale,
  Both mild and stale,
Should swim and float away.

And in the school
There was no rule
Throughout that summer's day;
  The boys, they could
  Not cross the flood,
And so,—they went to play.

But down it went,
Its force was spent
Before the close of day:
  Though strong and brisk
  The River Wiske,
It seem'd all *whisk'd* away.

And Farmer Brown
Rode through the town,
Right glad because his hay
  Was safe in pike
  Beyond the dyke,
And was not whisk'd away.

"Why, then, all's right,"
　Said old John White,
Whose hair was turn'd to grey:
"More fright than harm
　To stock or farm
The Wiske has brought to-day.

"And oft I think,
　As by its brink
To watch the waves I stray,
　So, like the moods
　Of summer floods,
Life's sorrows pass away."

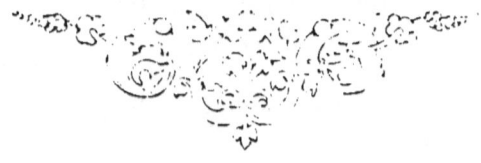

AD GULIELMUM MEUM.

Litteras, quas tu, Gulielme dulcis,
Lœtus et felix animi dedisti,
Lœtus accepi pater; est in illis
    Gratia chartis.

Acta cum charo patruo recenses;
Acta per terras recitas, marique,
Atque ubi pulchro novus enitescit
    Lumine lucus.*

Nactus es, mirande puer, magistrum,
Quem minus felix mihi sors negavit;
En viam, ut possis equitare, monstrat
    Doctus equiso.

Disce, sed ne prætuleris caballum,
Altius quamquam ingreditur, pusillæ,
Quae tuum assueta est equa ferre pondus.
    Optima equarum.†

---

* Anglicè, "Fairlight glen."
† Poeta commendat equam parvam Zetlandicam, Scoticè dictam "Wee Moggie."

AD GULIELMUM MEUM.

Illa, mannorum grege de pusillo,
Te manet pinguis reducem ; superba
Orcadum tellus patria est, vel ipsa
    Ultima Thule.

Hortulus floret tuus, et sororis ;
Hunc bonus custos coluit Johannes,
Ille qui nomen trahit a virentis
    Nomine bosci.*

        1846.

---

* Anglicè, "John Greenwood."

A LAY

TO THE

LAST MINSTREL

INSCRIBED TO THE MEMORY OF

SIR WALTER SCOTT.

"To guard a title which was rich before."—KING JOHN.

A LAY TO THE LAST MINSTREL.

"No one can make good his claim to be esteemed a noble poet, who is easy for everybody to understand, and who has not in him a good store of learned skill and knowledge of things, concealed beneath the surface." This is the expressed opinion of one who was himself a distinguished master of the art, and has borne among his countrymen the name of "the divine Herrera." * The question is whether Scott is an exception to this rule? But is not the answer to be found in the strange diversity of judgments formed about him and the creations of his pen, both during his life and since his death? This is not meant to refer to writers whose strong antipathies, moral or political, disqualify them from the capability of an unbiassed estimate, and have led them to speak of the great Minstrel as a hasty manufacturer of books for the purpose of making money and purchasing a landed estate; but we seem to have lived to hear men of more freedom of spirit, more unswayable by popular voices, and of some pretension to critical

---

* Escritos y Poesies ineditas; Sevilla, 1870, p. 86.

taste and learning, speak as if they thought the old admirers of those wonderful Lays and Romances wanted an apology. And, as Toryism is not at present in the sunshine, they intermix a little pity for the man who would not take his lesson in politics, in his last public appearance, from the weavers of Jedburgh, and wished to leave the old machine of State at rest, till it could be repaired by the best workman. Time will tell whether he was less wise than those who are now in the ascendant, whose policy is tending, with such admirable success, to resolve society into its primitive elements. But our business is not with Scott's politics, but his poetry.

To give to those who hint their doubts and hesitate their dislikes as high a support as they are likely to find elsewhere, it may be enough to refer to some disparaging remarks reported from the conversation of the Poet Wordsworth, which, if Wordsworth's true estimate of Scott had not, happily, been recorded by himself in his own undying verse, might leave an impression on the reader's mind as unjust to the one great poet as to the other. See *Memoir of Wordsworth*, vol. ii. 444. No doubt what may have fallen from the lips of such a man as Wordsworth, even in the course of casual conversation, must command respectful attention; but a report from memory of opinions expressed by him in talk cannot be received as evidence of his real estimate of Scott, when it is found to differ from his own deliberately-recorded testimony of his love and value for his brother-poet. That testimony has been given in no equivocal terms. What was Wordsworth's earliest impression of Scott's verse he has himself told us. When he first visited the minstrel at his home in the Border country, September 1803, Scott read to him a portion of the *Lay*. "The novelty of the manners," says Wordsworth, "the clear picturesque descriptions, and the ease and glowing energy of much of the verse, greatly delighted me." There is nothing in any of his subsequent writings to belie these early impressions. But there is still extant,—and it is not likely to be soon forgotten,—a poem which a good critic * has called "one of the finest occasional poems in the language," *Yarrow Revisited*. This poem, so deeply filled with affectionate veneration for Scott, and admiration for his diversified invention and power, Wordsworth himself valued so much, that a short time after the great minstrel's death he published another volume of his poems, with this to give it its leading title.† It would be a simple wrong to the memory of Wordsworth to suppose that he wrote this poem, or any other, in the style or spirit of those with whom "lowly feigning is called compliment."

---

* Mr. F. T. Palgrave.
† *Yarrow Revisited*, and other Poems, 1834; with a dedication to the Poet Rogers.

The observations ascribed to Wordsworth in conversation upon Scott as a poet were understood to apply only to such of his works as were literally in verse: but it is hardly conceivable that Wordsworth, a didactic philosopher in his own art and craft, should have adopted the vulgar technical distinction between prose and poetry, and have confined the minstrel's claim to be accounted a poet to his compositions in metre only. If he had forgotten his own doctrine of the identity of language in good poetry and well-written prose, could he have forgotten the enduring rule of the old master, that a poet establishes his title to the name rather by the construction of his plot and the conduct of his fable than by any skill in arranging syllables and metres? And must he not, in all likelihood, have read what another admirable poet had written in one of the most interesting and masterly critiques on the "Life and Writings of Sir Walter Scott," which has anywhere appeared?* "It is," says John Keble, "in his character as a great poet, as the leading one, that posterity will always consider him. His romances in prose are essentially poems, whatever test we take of poetry except that ordinary one of metre: indeed it would not, perhaps, be easy to find a completer proof of metrical composition being but an accident of the art, than any one can make out for himself, by recol-

---

* *British Critic*, October 1838.

lecting what he felt on first reading *The Lady of the Lake*, and how little the impression differed from that left by *The Talisman* or *Guy Mannering*. The kind of interest, the objects of sympathy, are surely the same in both cases: the difference of prose and verse is felt to be but technical; it is the same music performed on different instruments." And were not Ellen Douglas and her father, as well as Jeanie Deans or Caleb Balderstone, present to Wordsworth's mind when he penned to Scott the touching stanza:—

> "For thou, upon a thousand streams,
> By tales of love and sorrow,
> Of faithful love, undaunted truth,
> Hast shed the power of Yarrow"?

And was it not the *Lay*, above all, that clung to Wordsworth's memory, when, after climbing "the winding stair" of Newark Tower, he declared that "localised Romance" does *not* "play false with our affections"?

After this, it is hardly necessary to allude to a remark ascribed to him conveying the opinion that success is impossible in any attempt to represent the manners of a past time. Could he, who had so deep and true a sense of the high calling of the poet to sustain the heart of man amidst the changeful trials of the present with "visions of the past," have thought the poet powerless to give truth and life to those visions? Could he have forgotten Aristotle's distinction here also, that it is the historian's part to relate things as they were, the poet's to describe them as probably they might have been? Is the character of Louis XI. in *Quentin Durward* unlike the portrait presented to us in history? Does not the same degree of historical probability attach itself to the amusing soldier of fortune, Sir Dugald Dalgetty, in *The Legend of Montrose*, as belongs to the gallant Falconbridge in Skakspeare's *King John?* But such individual characters, each in his portion, embody the manners of past times.

Believing, therefore, that Wordsworth's real estimate of Scott is to be found in his own published words, rather than in any remarks reported from his conversation; believing this fully, as much for the credit of Wordsworth as of Scott, the present writer begs leave, in what will probably be his last appeal to an indulgent public, to pour forth a tribute of heartfelt homage to the Genius of Border Romance and Song. It is "Sixty years since," as a very young client of the Muses, he read *Marmion* in the first edition, stretched upon the grass, on a whole-holiday at school, and felt his heart melted by the benevolent wish in the greeting at the end, which how many thousands have since personally applied, and some few may still treasure in as long a grateful remembrance;

> " To thee, dear school-boy, whom my lay
> Has cheated of thy hour of play,
> Light task, and merry holiday!"

The chord then struck still vibrates with a pulse of gratitude and joy at the end of sixty years.

As to the fame of Scott, one may almost, without profaneness, take up St. Augustine's sentence of calm confidence for the safety of the Catholic Faith: *Securus judicat orbis terrarum.* With what truth as well as tenderness has Wordsworth called him "the whole world's darling"! The Germans number him among the few unapproached Englishmen of genius. The Italians are still among his most ardent admirers; and even in that land of poetry and romance, which gave birth to Cervantes and Calderon, his noble fictions were not only read in translations, but gave a tincture to the native novels of the day. "His name," says a generous Spaniard, "comes naturally to the memory and the lips, whenever we speak of Fernan Caballero."*

"It is not too much to say,"—to quote John Keble again,—"that never did any single writer exert a greater influence on his age." And, what he speaks of as then recent, it has been neither a slight nor a transient benefit " to have substituted his manly realities, both in prose and verse, for the flimsy enervating literature, which, with few exceptions, peopled the shelves of those who read chiefly for amusement." But there are some yet living to remember that his

---

* Don Manuel Camete. Prologo to Fernan Caballero's *Deudas Pagadas*, Madr. 1863.

reform extended to the language, as well as to the literature, of the time. He designed this, and was not unconscious of it, when he spoke of his own regard to the old Teutonic fountains of English undefiled.

When a modern German critic calls his poetry "Epic,"* he is not far wrong. The Epic of Homer grew out of the strains of the rhapsodists, much as the Lays and Tales of Scott were heroic structures built on the old foundations of the Border Ballad. And if Homer paints the manners of old Greece in prehistoric times, Scott's portraitures of feudal characters of the Middle Ages are as like the truth as they can be made on the evidence of historic probability. But with what masterly skill are the lines of his historic portraits drawn! Or rather, it is not so much the hand of the skilful artist, calmly studying the features he would represent, as the impulse of a bold actor, unchecked and unconstrained, throwing himself into the part which occupies the scene, and living in it, as Garrick or Siddons lived in the characters they sustained in their wondrous hours upon the stage.

One feature more requires to be noticed. It was the benevolent soul of Shakspeare and of Cervantes, opening itself to every kind impulse, loving humanity, as he beheld it, on its bright side, which gave Scott his power over all feeling hearts and minds. Who

---

* Herr Elze, quoted in *Quarterly Review*, Oct. 1871, p. 354.

would not have desired such a friend? Lockhart has well pointed out this in his apology,—if any one could think that an apology was needed,—for those delightful epistles prefixed to the several Cantos of *Marmion*. "It may be," he says, "that to a reader turning the leaves with the first ardour of curiosity, they may seem to interfere with the flow of the story. But however that may be, are there any pages, among all he ever wrote, that one would be more sorry he should not have written? They are among the most delicious portraitures that genius ever painted of itself,—buoyant, virtuous, happy genius—exulting in its own energies, yet possessed and mastered by a clear, calm, modest mind, and happy only in diffusing happiness around it." *

And this overflowing spirit of sympathy did not decline with years, or sink under his hard change of fortune. It was as much seen in *Anne of Geierstein* as in *Waverley*. With a man who wrote so much it is natural that there should have been great inequalities. There were poems, like *Harold the Dauntless*, struck off with a careless beat; and marks of haste, and characters less happily conceived, and scenes less probably worked up, in several of his romances; but the warm fancy was still alive, and ready to exert itself again with the happiest effect, when it was engaged with a

---

* Lockhart's *Life of Sir Walter Scott*, vol. ii. p. 151.

subject worthy of its powers, till the mortal tenement gave way, and the mind was clouded by the approaching shades of death. But he could then take comfort in the retrospect of his literary life with a reflection, surely not founded in self-conceit, that in all his voluminous writings "he had tried to unsettle no man's faith, to corrupt no man's principle, and had written nothing which on his deathbed he should wish to have blotted out."*

This Preface was written before making acquaintance with Principal Shairp's admirable essay on Wordsworth in his *Studies in Poetry and Philosophy*, or the very interesting article by the same author in *Good Words*, September 1873, on "Wordsworth's Three Yarrows;" but the present writer is glad to take this opportunity of expressing his grateful sense of the pleasure which both these papers have afforded him, especially in the just tribute there paid to the enduring friendship of the two great poets, "who," as Lockhart well observes, "had through life loved each other well, and in spite of very different theories as to art, appreciated each other's genius more justly than inferior spirits ever did either of them."†

---

* Scott's words to Mr. Edw. Cheney, in Lockhart's *Life*, vol. vii. p. 378.
† Lockhart's *Life of Scott*, vol. vii. p. 309.

A LAY TO THE LAST MINSTREL.

LINES WRITTEN AT DRYBURGH ABBEY,

September 3, 1860.

HE, who could burst with wizard rhyme
    The cells of joy and wonder,
The dungeons, where the miser Time
    Had stored his old world's plunder;

Who peopled rock-bound isle and glen,
    Brown heath, or lowland meadow,
With shadowy forms of godlike men,
    More glorious in their shadow;

Here rests in still Saint Mary's aisle
    With kindred dust departed,
Till the last dawn on earth shall smile,
    And waken bards true-hearted.

Tread softly, where thro' silent glades
    Soft evening dews are stealing,
Soft sunbeams slant, and nought invades
    The calm of holy feeling;

And Tweed upon his summer-flow,
   Through woodland mazes turning,
Hath hush'd his troubled voice of woe
   To sound of gentler mourning.

Ere yet the gracious hour be gone,
   Revere the dead, who slumbers,
Where with dumb spell the cold grey stone
   Hath bound his magic numbers.

—Nay, but those numbers, wandering free,
   Disdain a bed so narrow;
They breathe on many a breezy lea
   By Ettrick, Tweed, and Yarrow.

They live, they breathe: too fair for death,
   Fresh bloom of purple splendour
Invests the tales of love and faith,
   Of dauntless hearts and tender;

Fine fictions, veiling in her state
   The queenlike brow of Nature;
Sublime deceits, for truth too great,
   Yet vow'd to Truth as greater;

The days o'erpast, as Fancy wills,
   In golden hues portraying,
Bright as the morn on ancient hills
   When dewy gleams are straying.

They live,—the forms of ages gone,
    The merry drolls, whose gladness,
By cottage-hearth, or kingly throne,
    Unknit the brow of sadness;

Or shades of high heroic mood,
    Their wreaths in glory wearing,
Who stemm'd Rebellion's roaring flood,
    Or perish'd in the daring.

I see them yet: above, around,
    Bright spirits seem to linger;
To yon lone arch on holy ground
    They point with radiant finger;

And bid me, meditating still,
    Where dust in dust is lying,
Resolve what charm of potent skill
    Achieved that fame undying:

The genial wit, unforced by art,
    Through sportful sallies ranging;
Or more, that large and loyal heart,
    In love and faith unchanging;

The love, that, as the wakening child
    In smiling owns its mother,
On the stern land that nursed him, smiled,
    Nor joy'd in any other:

The faith, that to the faithful dead
    A life in memory giving,
Raised beacons to their worth, and led
    To noble deeds the living.

For this, while Britain's laws and throne
    Defend the soil that bore him,
His praise her sons of song shall own,
    And chaunt their requiem o'er him;

And gentle hearts his end shall know,
    How, like calm waves retreating,
The music of their full-voiced flow
    In dying falls repeating,

The spirit of the generous will
    Time's waning lamp attended,
Warm to his friend and country still,
    Till life and memory ended.

I've roam'd in thought, dark Florentine,
    With thee by Arno's water,
While keen remembrance fired each line
    With tales of kindred slaughter:

Or when thy lonely spirit felt
    Mild hope its peace infusing;
But scarcely love of kind could melt
    The sternness of thy musing.

I've roam'd in sunny lands of Spain,
 By sunny memories haunted
Of him, whose gravely mirthful vein
 From fables disenchanted,

And chased away, with smiling glee,
 Grim Folly's old disorder;*
But could not cheer the heart like thee,
 Dear Minstrel of the Border.

Bright roll the brooks down Arno's vale,
 Bright gleams the darting Darro;
But more to me the shadows pale
 By Tweed and pensive Yarrow.

---

* Scott said of the great Florentine, " It is mortifying that Dante seemed to think nobody worth being sent to the Inferno but his own Italians; whereas other people had as great rogues in their own families."—Lockhart's *Life of Scott*, vii. 371. The narrator, from whom the biographer received this remark, gives it a more humorous application. But it seems to me that our warm-hearted Minstrel found the heroic indignation of Dante against so many of his own kith and kin rather difficult and uncongenial to him.

On the other hand, as one might well have supposed, he was thoroughly at home with Cervantes. "He expressed the most unbounded admiration for him, and said that his 'Novelas' had first inspired him with the ambition of excelling in fiction; and that, until disabled by illness, he had been a constant reader of them."—*Ibid.* 370. He read them, it is scarcely necessary to add, in the original Spanish.

TRANSLATIONS AND IMITATIONS.

FROM THE LATIN.

VEXILLA REGIS.

The banners of our King go forth,
    The sacred Cross is beaming high;
Whereon the Lord of heaven and earth
    Endured a sinner's death to die;

Where the rude spear, whose baleful steel
    Fulfill'd the soldier's ruthless mood,
Reveal'd a Fount to cleanse and heal,
    Pure Water and atoning Blood.

Then were the wonders plainly shown,
    Which saints of old rejoiced to sing,
How of the Tree He made a Throne,
    Whereby He reign'd a glorious King.

O ever bright and beaming Tree,
    With purple of our King array'd,
How great thy glory, that on thee
    Those limbs of holiest power were laid!

O blest by every faithful tongue,
    Whereon, the sinners' debt to pay,
The weight of this world's ransom hung
    And spoil'd the spoiler of his prey.

Hail to the Cross, whereon He bled,
    But more to Him the Victim slain;
Our Life, Who bow'd to death His head
    By death our endless life to gain!

SALVETE, FLORES MARTYRUM.

Hail, young flowers of martyrdom,
    Whom the ruthless sword hath shorn ;
Rosebuds, in your morning's bloom
    By the deadly whirlwind torn :

You the Lord, for Whom ye bled,
    Firstlings of His flock shall own ;
Lambs, who play'd, to slaughter led,
    Sporting with your palms and crown.

What avails the murderer's knife?
    What hath cruel Herod found?
Christ is borne beyond that strife
    Where no tyrant's sword can wound.

While His infant mates lie low,
    While the childless mothers mourn,
One hath 'scaped the reaver's blow,
    One, of Maiden Mother born.

Praise and glory be address'd
    Jesu, Virgin-born, to Thee :
Father, Son, and Spirit blest,
    Praise we everlastingly.

FROM THE ANGLO-SAXON.

THE RESURRECTION.

FROM CAEDMON.

Dim and dark Death's shadow lay
On the abode of woe that day,
When, upborne to earth afar,
Rose our Bright and Morning Star,
Rose th' Eternal Lord of men.
Crowds of faithful spirits then
Of the race of Abraham old
Seers, who erst that day foretold,
Mustering their triumphant bands
Bore the Victor in their hands,
Bore Him as His guard of state
Fast to Salem's city-gate.
For the conquest now was won,
Ere the promise of the sun;
Ere the midnight watch gave way
To the ruddy dawn of day.
Then the thunder-peal from heaven
Death's strong bars had burst and riven,
And with lightning mark'd the road
Of the First-born Son of God.

FROM KING ALFRED.

Ne'er may man on mountain crest
    Rear his roof-tree fast to bide;
Nor will Wisdom build her nest
    In the rocking winds of pride;

Ne'er the shifting sands may give
    Seat assured for house or hall;
Nor with thee will Wisdom live,
    If base earth thy soul enthrall.

Bare and barren sands, whose thirst
    Weltering rain-floods ne'er can fill,—
Such the man, whose soul is cursed
    With the unsated worldling's will.

Would'st thou for thyself prepare
    Bliss that shall be aye thine own?
Fly, O fly the false world's glare;
    Fix thy lowly corner-stone,

Where at peace thy gentle mind
    With itself at home may dwell;
Where no floods, nor bitter wind,
    Can remove the hallow'd cell.

FROM THE ANGLO-SAXON.

When the storm clouds, sweeping by
    Vex th' unquiet welkin round,
Vainly shall their fury try
    To disturb that charmèd ground;

For the hollow *dene* each day
    By immortal feet is trod;
Wisdom meets thee on thy way,
    And it is th' abode of God.

FRAGMENT FROM THE ANGLO-SAXON METRICAL CALENDAR.

Seven nights ere December end
Did the Sire of Angels send
Comfort far and wide to earth
In his Son's, our Saviour's, birth.
'Twas the bleak mid-winter's morn,
When that mighty King was born,
Christ, the Glory-King of heaven,
And to Him a Name was given,
Jesus, Healer of all woes,
When the eighth day's light arose;
E'en that selfsame morning, when
Busy crowds of happy men
Meet rejoicing far and near
In the birth-day of the year.
For to town that self-same day
Still a stranger takes his way,
Foremost still at morn he's there;
'Tis the month hight January,
Porter to the Calendar.
Then, when five long nights are gone,
Twelfth's day holy morn comes on,

Our blest King's baptismal day,
His, who wash'd our sins away.
Noblest chiefs of British mould
Still that day in reverence hold.

When four weeks are almost flown,
Wanting yet two nights alone,
Comes the little FEBRUARE,
When the sun, returning fair,
Lengthens our brief winter day.
Laws of ancient wisdom, say,
Is it not as I declare.
Of the little Februare?
But when one night more shall pass,
Comes the Blessed Mary's mass,
Mother of our Heavenly King:
'Tis the day that she did bring
To the solemn Temple's floor
Him whom heaven and earth adore.
Five nights more, and Winter goes;
Then add seventeen nights to those,
And the Saint's day comes, whose breath
Then was yielded up in death
For the Saviour whom he loved,
Great Matthias, well approved:
Near the time when, far and wide
Christians keep their Lenten tide.

Well 'tis known, when three and twain
Waning nights are past again,
Save when once in twelvemonths four
Leap-year makes it one night more,
Churl or carl by dale or down
Feel that MARCH is come to town,
Wrathful March in blustering mood:
Loud his voice by strand or flood,
And his beard bespangled o'er
With the rime of hail-show'rs hoar.
When eleven nights are past,
Then, on Time's wing flying fast,
Comes the solemn memory nigh
Of the blessed Gregory,
Famous for God's holy lore
Sent to Britain's isle of yore.
And when nine more days are gone
Holy Bennet's day comes on:
Then his Saviour's rest he sought,
Stedfast in the rules he taught:
Well extoll'd in writings wise
By the goodly companies
Who, like soldiers formed in line,
March beneath his discipline.
Then, as reckoners teach aright,
Even space of day and night
Holds dominion o'er the earth:
For the Lord of Nature's birth

Then first set their course to run
Evermore both moon and sun.
What is next to tell? The day,
When four nights have pass'd away,
When th' Eternal Father sent
From the crystal firmament
His high angel, news to bring
How heaven's Ever-Blessed king
Should of Mary mild be born :
Sinful earth, that lay forlorn
Never yet such tidings heard
As were in that mighty word.

Days and nights pass four and three,
And in season orderly
APRIL, changeful month, is here ;
Then most oft the varying year
Brings the tide of greatest joy,
Bliss that foe can ne'er destroy,
Comfort of all mortal woes ;
'Tis the tide when Christ arose,
As of old the prophet said,
'Tis the day the Lord hath made,
Day of consecrated mirth
To the happy sons of earth.
But unfix'd is that high Day ;
Nor more certainly we may

Reckon when the Lord ascended,
When His work on earth was ended,
For it varieth evermore :
But the wise in starry lore
Every year by skilful ways
Find these solemn holy-days.

Shall we pass unheedful by
The good martyrs' memory ?
Let our song record the day ;
Ere glad Easter's moon decay,
When the nineteenth night is gone,
Then the solemn tide comes on.
'Tis a famous day of prayer :
When their relics men up-rear,
Oft in glittering caskets set,
Where the gazing crowds are met.
Then with mirth in field and bower,
Comes bright MAY's rejoicing hour.

FROM ALDHELM'S PSALTER.*

Psalm LXXXIV. 1-5.

Lord, to me thy minsters are
Courts of honour, passing fair;
And my spirit deems it well
There to be, and there to dwell:
Heart and flesh would fain be there,
Lord, Thy life, Thy love to share.

There the sparrow speeds her home,
And in time the turtles come,
Safe their nestling young they rear,
Lord of hosts, Thine altars near;
Dear to them Thy peace;—but more
To the souls who there adore.

---

* This and the following Anglo-Saxon poems are from the *Early English Church*.

Psalm LXVIII. 11-13.

God the word of wisdom gave;
   Preachers, who his voice have heard,
Taught by Him, in meekness brave,
   Speed the message of that word.
Mighty King with beauty crown'd!
   In His House the world's proud spoil,
Oft in almsdeeds dealt around,
   Cheers the poor wayfarer's toil.
If among His clerks you rest,
   Silver plumes shall you enfold,
Fairer than the culver's breast,
   Brighter than her back of gold.

Psalm XCIII. 3, 4.

When the tempest wakes to wrath
    Many waters wide and far,
On the ocean's dreadful path
    Loud and high their voices are:
Wondrous ways those waters move,
    Where the sea-streams swiftest flow;
But more wondrous far above,
    Holy Lord, Thy glories show.

Psalm CXVI. 15.

As the beacon-fire by night,
    That the host of Israel led,
Such the glory, fair and bright,
    Round the good man's dying bed:
'Tis a beacon bright and fair,
Telling that the Lord is there.

METRICAL PARAPHRASE OF THE APOSTLES' CREED.

FATHER of unchanging might,
Set above the welkin's height,
Who the unsullied tracts of air
Didst in their own space prepare,
And the solid earth as fast
With its deep foundations cast,—
Thee, the Everlasting One,
With believing heart I own.
Life itself from Thee had birth,
Lord of angels, King of earth;
Thou the ocean's mighty deep
In its pathless caves dost keep;
And the countless stars that glow,
Thou their power and names dost know.
 And with faith assured I own
Lord, Thy true and only Son,
King of might to heal and save;
Whom Thy pitying mercy gave
Hither for our help to come
From the blissful angels' home.
Gabriel, on Thine errand sent,
Through the crystal firmament

Glancing with the speed of thought,
Thy behest to Mary brought.
She, the Virgin pure and blest,
Freely bow'd to Thy behest,
And the Father's wondrous power
Praised in that rejoicing hour.
There no earth-born lust had room;
Spotless was that Maiden's womb,
As a casket meet to bear
Brightest gem, heav'n's first-born heir.
But such bliss as Angels know
Thy pure Spirit did bestow;
And the Maid and Mother mild
Gave to earth her heaven-born Child,
Born as man, our needs to prove,
Maker of the hosts above!
Heavenly comfort, at His birth,
Dawn'd upon the sons of earth;
And by David's lowly town
Angels brought glad tidings down,
That the Healer of all woe
Sojourn'd now with men below.

    Then, when under men of Rome
Pilate held the power to doom,
Our dear Lord gave up His breath,
Bore the bitter throes of death
On the rood as sinners die,
King of endless majesty!

Sadly Joseph made His grave
In his own sepulchral cave:
But His soul was gone to quell
Foes that held the spoil of hell
In the fiery cells that keep
Spirits long imprison'd deep,
Whom His summons call'd away
To their home in upper day.

Then when came the third day's light
Rose again the Lord of might;
Freshly from His clay-cold bed
King of light and life He sped.
Forty days His followers true
To His heavenly lore He drew,
Holy *runes* * unfolding, ne'er
Heard before by mortal ear;
Till His hour to reign was come,
And He sought His glorious home:
But His promise left to man,
From the hour that reign began,
That no more distraught with dread
Faithful men His ways should tread;
But with patience standing fast
Of His free deliverance taste.

I the Spirit of all grace
With unswerving faith embrace,

---

* *Runes*, mysteries; alluding to Acts i. 3.

Whom the tongues of nations own,
With the Father and the Son,
Everlasting GOD. Though Three
Named by Name, yet One they be:
One the Godhead, One alone,
Whom in differing names we own.
Faith receives the mystery,
Yielding truth the victory.
Wheresoe'er the world is spread,
Lord, Thy glory-gifts are shed,
To Thy saints in wonders shown;
And eternal is Thy Throne.
Furthermore, I keep and hold
Ever-loved of God, the Fold
Of His faithful ones, that are
Ever the good Shepherd's care,
That true Church, that to heaven's King
Doth accordant praises sing:
And the fellowship bestow'd
On the saints in earth's abode,
With the souls that dwell with God.

Free forgiveness for each sin
Penitent I hope to win:
And with faith assured, I trust
That this flesh, return'd to dust,
Shall arise, with all the dead,
At the day of doom and dread;

When our endless state shall be,
Judge of all men, fix'd by Thee,
As on earth our works are still
Measured by our Maker's will.

VERSES REPEATED BY THE VENERABLE BEDE.

Ere the pilgrim soul go forth
   On its journey far and lone,
Who is he that yet on earth
   All his needful part hath done?

Who foreweighs the joy and scathe
   That his parted ghost shall know,
Endless, when the day of death
   Seals his doom for weal or woe?

FROM THE BRETON.

(See *Barzaz-Breiz. Chants populaires de la Bretagne. De la Villemarqué.*—Paris, 1846.)

THE DEATH-SONG OF GWENC'HLAN.

As sets the sun I chaunt my lay, while swells the sounding sea,
Here at the door I sit and sing, but all is dark to me.
I sang in youth, I sing in age, as I was wont of yore;
I sing by night, I sing by day, and yet my grief is sore:
Low sinks this head that once was high: my heart is full of woe;
Oh not without a weighty cause my head and heart are low.
It is not that I fear to die; I fear not to be slain,
I fear not: life was sweet; but now I would not live again.
A time will come, when all unsought my presence men shall find;
But now departing, like a cloud, I leave no trace behind.

No matter,—what must come will come,—to mourn
    or to be blest,
Three deaths in life must all men die, ere comes life's
    final rest.

II.

I see the wild boar from the wood; he halts, his feet
    are sore:
His bristly crest is white with age; his jaws are red
    with gore.
Around him throng his boarish brood: grim Famine
    prowling nigh
Preys on their wasted flanks; their hour is come, and
    they must die.
I see the sea-horse on the deep; a terror shakes the
    shore:
White is his form as sparkling snow; with silvery
    horns before.
The briny spray is boiling round, his thundering
    nostrils glow:
His army's ranks are close as reeds where silent waters
    flow.
Hold on, hold on, thou sea-horse fierce, and strike
    the monster's head!
Blood on the ground! bare feet may slip on footing
    dark and red;

Blood like a river! Blood knee-deep! Strike home! again strike home!
Blood like a sea! strike the death-stroke! to-morrow rest will come.

III.

While I was softly sleeping in my cold and tomb-like cell,
At midnight deep I heard the call, the famish'd eagle's yell:
She call'd her roving eaglets all, she call'd the tribes of air:
"Mount, mount on wing," aloud she cried, "the feast of death to share;
'Tis not the flesh of murrain-sheep, or corpse of mangled hound:
I snuff the scent of Christian blood, a chieftain's mortal wound."
—Tell me, thou grey one from the sea, old raven, oft hast thou
On morsels from War's table fed: say what thy banquet now?
"I hold," she cries, "the chieftain's skull, it is my choice to dine
With beak-thrusts on his cruel eyes, whose wrath extinguish'd thine."

—Tell me, grey fox, what prize is that which war to thee hath thrown?

"I hold and rend his knavish heart, heart falser than mine own,

That plann'd and panted for thy death long since, thy death of pain."

—Thou toad, that watchest at his lip, what dost thou wait to gain?

"I wait to catch his parting soul, in vengeance doom'd to be

In durance all my lengthen'd age a captive pent in me.

Thus be avenged the Bard he wrong'd, the lays beloved of men,

The voice no longer heard between Roch-allaz and Porz-gwenn."

JOAN DE MONTFORT.

What strange flock, at nightfall seen,
Climbs the mountain's deep ravine?
Mountain-sheep upon their track?
Mountain-sheep were ne'er so black.
'Tis a troop of armed Franks:
Swift they come in silent ranks,
To besiege with all their power
Hennebont's guarded town and tower.

But the duchess, wise and ware,
Eyes the foe and mocks the snare:
Cheerily the loud bells sound
While she rides the fortress round.
'Twas a sight of pride to see,
When, her babe upon her knee,
On her palfrey white she rode;
And where'er she came, the crowd
Raised on high their cries of joy:
" God defend her and her boy!
God defend her!" was the cry:
" Let the knavish Frenchmen die."

Vaunting ere they took their prey,
You might hear those Frenchmen say,

"We shall catch them, as on lawn
   Hunters catch both hind and fawn :
   Golden chains shall bind in one
   Both the mother and the son."
From her towers the Duchess heard,
And her noble wrath was stirr'd :
"Nay, you'll catch no hind in lair ;
   Let the prowling wolf* beware ;
   If to-night he shake with cold,
   Royally we'll warm his hold."

From the towers whereon she stood
Down she came in wrathful mood ;
Not with silken head-band now,
But with casque upon her brow ;
Not with velvet boddice laced,
But with corselet on her waist :
Glittering steel of proof she wore,
And a keen-edged sword she bore.
From her host for battle then
Straight she chose three hundred men,
Seized a firebrand, and in haste
Through an angle gate she pass'd.

Lo! the Frenchmen, close in tent
With their weary march forespent,

---

* A play on the name of her enemy, Charles de Blois, here called *Bleiz*, the Breton word for *wolf*.

Held their revels gay and long,
Startling Night's dull ear with song';
When a voice with stranger lay
Broke upon those revels gay:
" More than one who laughs to-night,
Shall be sad ere dawning light';
He who eats the bread so white,
Soon the cold black dust shall bite:
He who pours the red wine good
Soon shall pour his heart's best blood.
He who brags, of nought afraid,
Shall on ashy bed be laid."
While e'en yet, half drunken dead,
On the board lean'd many a head,
Rose a cry of terror, higher
Than the songs and laughter, "Fire!"
" Fly, oh fly! the flames rush on,
'Tis the hand of Fiery Joan!"

Yes! full sure, Joan's fiery hand
First and foremost hurl'd the brand,
Hurl'd it in the darkest hour,
Hurl'd it on the corners four,
Set the French camp all alight;
Fierce the glare and murk the night!
Tents and men were wrapp'd in fire,
Night-winds sped the burning dire;

Of three thousand men who came
Scarce five-score survived that flame.

Fiery Joan, when morn arose,
Did her lattice high unclose;
O'er the scene with wrecks defiled
Grimly did she gaze, and smiled;
While the smouldering embers lay
Pale beneath the new-born day.
Grimly did she smile, and said:
"Ha, good clearance has been made!
Clearance for the plough; the field
Shall a tenfold increase yield.
Well our elders said of yore,
When their battle day was o'er:
'Would ye see fair corn-crops grown,
  Spread good store of Gaulish bone!'"

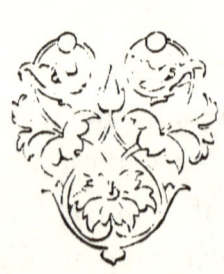

FROM THE CATALAN.

See *Observaciones sobre la Poesia popular*, etc.: *Mila y Fontanals.*—Barcelona, 1853. *Romancero General: Agustin Duran.*—Madrid, 1851. *Los Trobadors Nous: Ant. de Bofarull.*—Barcelona, 1858.

COUNT ARNALDOS.

Who had e'er so strange a fortune
    O'er the deep seas rolling on
As befel the Count Arnaldos
    On the morning of Saint John?

Forth he rode to chase at dawning,
    With his falcon on his hand,
When he saw a stately galley
    Working onward to the strand;

With silken sails that glisten'd
    On the cordage fine and strong;
And the helmsman at the rudder
    Chaunted still a wondrous song.

At his voice the sea in stillness
    Like a silver mirror lay,
And the winds with lowly whisper
    Softly kiss'd the silent bay.

And the fish that haunt the hollows
    Rose upon the deep's calm floor;
On the mast the sea-birds resting
    Wing'd the mid-way air no more.

" My galley, O my galley,
    God shield thee well for me,
From the false world and its dangers,
    O'er the waters of the sea.

" From the shoals of Almeria,
    From Gibraltar's rock-bound coast,
From Venetian Gulf, and Flanders
    Where the lives on sands are lost,—

" And the stormy Gulf of Lyons,
    Where pain the shipmen drie,
Where most of all the tempest
    Wakes the dangers of the sea !"

Then spake the Count Arnaldos,
    And oh, his prayer was strong:
" In the name of God, good seaman,
    Let me learn thy wondrous song."

The mariner made answ
" Alas ! it may not be :
That song,—no mortal learn,
Except he sail with me."

This Ballad has been already well rendered into English verse by Lockhart and by Archbishop Trench. It is also the subject of Longfellow's *Secret of the Sea*.

THE SOLDAN'S DAUGHTER.

It was the Soldan's Daughter,
  When springtide deck'd the bowers,
Her simple mind full fain would know
  The Lord of all the flowers:

To her the Lord of flowers
  In vision did appear:
"My heart," He said, "is warm'd to thee
  Thy gentle vow to hear:

"Take, take these crimson roses,
  Their hue was found in Me,
When Love in death all bleeding lay,
  The Love that died for thee.

"I hear My Father calling:
  Beloved, espoused one, come;
Long since thou wast ordain'd to reign
  Where flowers immortal bloom."

She heard: her spirit trusted
  The Voice till then unknown,
And meekly for the Lord of flowers
  She twined the rosy crown.

THE STRANGER CHILD ON CHRISTMAS EVE.

'Tis Yule-tide, and the blessed night
    When happy children meet,
And every hearth is warm and bright,
    And silent every street;

Save where one little wanderer comes,—
    His eyes are pale and wild,—
Homeless amidst a thousand homes;
    It is the Stranger-Child.

He shivers in the cold night air;
    He hears the mirth and glee:
"The Christmas-joy is everywhere,
    For all,—but not for me."

Lo! from afar, approaching now,
    In vesture pure and white,
A glory round His gracious brow,
    And in His hand a light,

Another Child comes down the street:
    His mien is sad and grave;
But oh, His voice is low and sweet,
    Like music on the wave.

"Weep not," He said, " thou Stranger-Boy:
  For thee there yet is room,—
Room in My Father's hall of joy:
  My light shall guide thee home."

Led by that light, a happy guest,
  The wondering Child is gone:
But who hath seen the home of rest
  Which Love hath made his own?

THE PRISONERS OF LERIDA.

In prison-house at Lerida, there lay in prison strong
Five-score and fifty captive men, who sang their captive song.
A lady to the lattice came, a lady fair and young:
The captives were aware of her, and ceased their captive song.
"Why sing ye not, poor captive men? why check your pleasant song?"
"O lady, how should captives sing, who lie in prison strong,
With morsel poor and bever scant, and all but once a day?
Look in and see our meagre fare, and bear it as you may."
"Sing on, sing on, poor captive men: for I will mend it soon."
She went to find her father dear, to beg of him a boon.
"How now, my daughter Margaret? what boon should I give thee?"
"O father dear, sweet father dear, the key, the prison-key!"

"Ah no, my daughter Margaret: in faith it may not be:
To-morrow morn those captive men must hang on gallows-tree."
"O father dear, and wilt thou hang the youth who sued to me?"
"Alas! my daughter Margaret, but prythee, which is he?"
"O father dear, my father dear, the ruddiest and most tall."
"Alas! my daughter! he must hang the foremost of them all."
"O father dear, my father dear, I pray thee, hang me too."
"O no, my daughter Margaret, such deed I may not do."
The gallows were with silver deck'd, the ropes with gold were twined;
On every beam a wreath of flowers waved sweetly in the wind;
And every passer-by, who snuff'd the fragrance in the air,
For that poor lover doom'd to death sent up a silent prayer.

(Variation, which may be added.)

That night her father slept full sound: she took the prison-key:

"Go forth, go forth, poor captive men, care not to stay for me;
Haste, haste to France; if well you speed, you'll there indite a song,
How once Don Jayme's daughter saved your lives from prison strong."
O then they leap'd and ran like men who felt that free they were;
One only linger'd at the gate, the youth who sued to her.

DON JUAN AND DON RAYMOND.

Young Juan and young Raymond rode glad to chase
    at morn;
But oh, the change, the heavy change! the woe of
    their return!
First from his horse Don Raymond fell, Don Juan
    drooping rode,
Their mother mark'd them as they came, in verdant
    field abroad,
A lady-leech, she gather'd there the balm and violet,
To heal the hurts their steeds might bear, if saddle-bow
    should fret.
"What aileth thee, son Raymond? thy face is wan
    and pale."
"O mother, lay me soon to sleep; they've bled me
    to my bale."
"Oh, ill betide the barber-leech, whose lancet did the
    harm!"
"Nay, mother, trouble not thy heart; but, past all
    herb or charm,
My life is ebbing to its fount; no more with joy and
    pride
Shall I in tourney or in chase my gallant courser
    ride.

Between my steed and me, strong lance-thrusts twenty-nine
We bode,—the nine my brave horse took, and all the rest were mine.
My gallant horse will die to-night, who me so well hath borne,
My gallant horse will die to-night, and I to-morrow morn.
My horse! Oh choose him well a place beneath the stable floor,
And let his burial be the best, who me so bravely bore.
And me, for me must grave be made in vaulted holy ground,
In Saint Eulalia's holy aisle; my sires are sleeping round;
And on my tomb a sword laid out shall mark the solemn place,
And if men ask, who caused my death,—" Don Juan on the chase."

THE COUNT OF ERIL.

Home rode the Count of Eril at early dawn of day;
Full many a moon had wax'd and waned, while he was far away.
An aged liegeman met his lord hard by his castle-gate,
"Oh whither now, my noble Count, so early, yet so late?"
"I come to see my lady, too long by me unseen."
"Ah, noble lord, thy lady is as she had never been.
I heard the solemn chaunt and prayer, when she was lowly laid;
I saw the palace-hangings in mourning pomp array'd;
I saw amidst the funeral train the blooming boys she bore,
Too young their loss to know, or why the mourner's dress they wore."
The good Count answer'd not again, but onward urged his way;
He sought her tomb and challenged Death to yield him back his prey;
With sword-point on the mound he call'd, strong love o'er-mastering fear,
"Rise, rise, my lady sweet, oh rise; thy only lord is here."

Did fancy wake, or Mercy send a dream to soothe
  his pain?
A voice seem'd issuing from the tomb, and answer'd
  him again:
"How can I rise, good Count? not thus can I return
  to thee.
Oh wed another bride, good Count, and wed for love
  of me.
And the lady of thy second choice, let her be to thee
  as I;
In thought of her the thought of me will evermore be
  nigh.
And for our little children, till they come to man's
  estate,
Let their young life be shielded well within the con-
  vent-gate.
Of the world, and what it means, let them hear no
  mention there,
But learn at eventide and morn to lisp their Saviour's
  prayer."

BALLAD OF THE WAR OF THE SUCCESSION.—CIRCA 1704.

WILL you hear what a fortune
    A gipsy wife told
To King Louis's grandson,
    Of courage so bold,
When he set out from Paris
    To king it in Spain?
"Farewell, my lord Duke,
    Till we see you again!

"Your hand if you'll give me
    I soon shall divine
What destiny waits you
    By reading each line;
I can weigh in true balance
    Your loss and your gain;
Farewell, my lord Duke
    Till we see you again!

"Here's a cross in the palm,
    Boding trouble and toil;
Many tossings and crossings
    Of angry turmoil

In the racket of Fortune
   You'll have to sustain;
Farewell, my lord Duke,
   Till we see you again!

" You have sworn you will reign;
   But the little bird sings
That saying and doing
   Are different things.
By right or by wrong
   You have sworn you will reign :—
Farewell, my lord Duke,
   Till we see you again!

" When you reach Barcelona
   Your Court you will hold
In the land of the Catalans
   Forward and bold,
The dread of your Gascons'
   So vaunting and vain;
Farewell, my lord Duke,
   Till we see you again!

" A young bride of Savoy
   Both blooming and fair,
Like gold in the sunlight
   The rays of her hair,

You shall wed, and be thankful
    She pities your pain;
But still, my lord Duke,
    We shall see you again.

"Your Queen's wit and beauty
    Will tell in the scale
With the lords of Castille,
    But it may not avail.
The balance will turn
    To a prince of Almaine;
And then, my lord Duke,
    We shall see you again.

"Those Catalan fellows,—
    I hear the bird sing,—
Will fight for Don Carlos,
    And make him their king.
For him they will battle
    With might and with main:—
Farewell, my lord Duke!
    We shall see you again!

"You fain would chastise
    In the French braggart style
Those Catalan lads:
    But be patient awhile!

Barcelona will scatter
　　That dream from your brain :
Farewell, my lord Duke,
　　Till we see you again !

" Then in Guadalajara
　　Your rival you'll face,
At the head of your troops ;
　　Nay, you'll fly in disgrace.
Though 't were time then or never
　　Your cause to maintain,
You will fly, my lord Duke,
　　We shall see you again !

" For King Charles will be there,
　　And Navarre will come down
With powder and bullets
　　To fight for his crown ;
Such a dance they will lead you,
　　You'll never draw rein
Till you come to Versailles
　　A true Frenchman again.

" Pretenders are many,
　　Great leaders are few ;
When you die, in your will
　　You'll dispose of Anjou,

And your silver that's left
   From your travels in Spain:
Farewell, my lord Duke,
   Till we see you again!

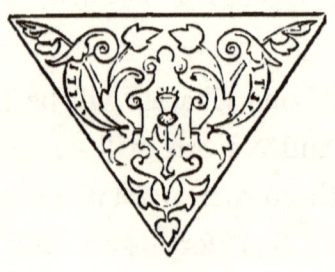

THE DEATH OF BACH DE RODA

FRANCISCO M. BACH DE RODA was a gallant Catalan, who, in the War of the Succession, took a forward part in the struggle against the French party, which was so stoutly maintained in his native province. The fervent provincial-patriotism of the hero, and the deep resentful sympathy of his compatriots, as expressed in this contemporary ballad, are thoroughly characteristic of Catalonia.

FAREWELL, thou cruel town of Vich,—a burning were
    thy meed:
The noblest knight of all thy plain thy wrath has
    doom'd to bleed,
Francisco Bach, of Roda town, the noble and the
    brave.
Saint Mary, and Saint Dominic, O where were ye
    to save?
O where were ye on that sad day, when holy clerks
    proclaim
The graces of the Rosary, and Carmel's saintly name?
In friendship's guise foul Treason came: they bade
    him to descend
His chamber stairs; a friend required the service of
    a friend.

Scarce had he reach'd the floor, when fast with cords his arms they tied,
And on a sledge at horse's tail to Vich they made him ride.
And now was proclamation made: "All carpenters, attend,
Come forth and build new gallows-trees right at the High Street end."
The carpenters and builders said, "We have no wood in store,
Wrought for the work." "Then break the posts and frames around each door."
They break them, and the chandeliers and lamps of silver bright
They bear away to guide their steps through darkness of the night.
Then loud the crier proclaim'd again, "Close fast each city-gate."
They shut them: thus the pardon sent, excluded, came too late.
They seize him now, and bind again, and bear to gallows-tree.
There on the platform high he stood, and those last words spake he:
"They doom me dead, but for no wrong,—no treason-guilt have I:
No troop of bandits have I led; no felon's death I die.

But for my country's weal I stood: her weal most
dear to me:
For her defence I took the sword, and pray'd God
set her free.
To Raymond, my good ghostly sire, I give this box
of gold,
To keep in memory of me when I am dead and cold.
And now no qualms of death I feel: nay, death is
most my friend.
One task undone alone I leave; it haunts me to the
end.
My daughters three are all betrothed:—Heaven bless
their marriage-bed!
This grieves me in my sudden fate,—I cannot see
them wed!"

THE DOUBTFUL PROMISE.

There be maidens in the city, and beyond the town likewise,
Maidens of the pleasant suburbs; early in the dawn they rise:
Early as the larks at sunrise, in the morning's ruddy glow,
You may see them wash their aprons and their apron-strings also.
Then by chance a fine young wooer walks to take the morning air,
And he stops to see the laundry, thinks it wise to loiter there:
"Damsel, give me a love-token: let no scorn the boon deny."
"Granted! shall it be my shoe-string, or my bonny apron-tie?"
"Fie upon it! not your shoe-string, nor your apron-girdle, no!
But a love-knot of those roses round your porch that twine and blow."
"Come upon St. Peter's even, when the summer day is gone.
Come at even on St. Peter's, or the matins of St. John:

Come, as now, at early morning, when you hear the matin bells,
Then the roses will be blooming—for yourself or some one else."

THE WOMAN'S-TAILOR'S LOVE.

The highland maids of Canigo,—so bright in bower and hall
All summer there they flourish fair, in spring, and autumn-fall:
One little damsel there I saw,—'twas but in passing by:
My heart she holds in golden chains that never will untie.
I went to drink the fountain cool, where sweet the waters rise;
And while I took the grateful draught, I heard soft tears and sighs:
It was herself, all sad at heart, that little love of mine:
"How shall I find a dear new dress, with skirts and boddice fine?"
"O soon the fair-day will be here,—the fairing shall be thine;
And I will buy the flowery skirt, the skirt and boddice fine.
But say, what colour pleaseth thee, my pretty Queen of May?"
"O friend, the crimson likes me best, it is so brave and gay."

The tailor loved my lovely one; he plied his willing powers,
And every braid his needle made he trimm'd with sprigs of flowers;
And oft he sigh'd, that not his own, but Fate's preventive shears
Forbade his slender thread of life to be entwined with hers.

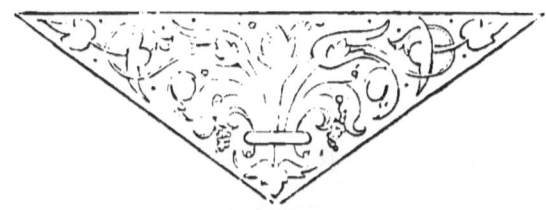

"WITH CONSENT."

'Twas on a fresh May morning, I took my dog and gun :
But game to shoot I found not,—of old my luck was none.
A little shepherd maiden beneath a beechwood tree
Was sleeping where her sheep and lambs were wandering o'er the lea.
A handful of the violet-flowers I gathered, and in play
I threw them on the maiden's neck in slumbers as she lay.
The violet-flowers were fresh and sweet,—she woke : —I see her stand
E'en now, as then she stood and spake, her distaff in her hand :
"What make you here, young master? what would you seek or find?"
"Your love, my pretty maiden,—let but your heart be kind."
"Go, ask it of my father, and ask it of my mother ;
Go, ask it of the tall young man who calls himself my brother :

Go, ask it of my maiden aunt,—she says she loves
   me well :
And my uncle dear, the chaplain,—you'll find him
   at his cell.
And if all five agree in one, you'll then be in the
   road ;
For, past all doubt, with five consents, I shall be well
   bestow'd."

GOOD NIGHT AT MALLORCA.

Long is the night to him that waketh,
    Short is the night when sleep is sound:
God grant us joy when morning breaketh,
    God send us rest while night goes round.

Soft as on bed of down new-driven
    Sweet sleep with heart at rest be mine;
And life, new life, shall dawn from heaven,
    When morn's first eastern ray shall shine.

Look up, my soul! thy God is near thee,
    Who clothes the fields and guards each flower
That blooms or fadeth: He shall hear thee
    In joy or sorrow's heaviest hour.

Thy drooping hope again shall flourish,
    The good day dimm'd shall shine again;
The times of tears more richly nourish
    Fresh seeds of gladness sown in pain.

Hast thou done well? O never, never
    Is goodness in this world alone:
A friend is thine no change can sever,
    Thy true heart, evermore thy own.

An orphan thou mayst mourn to-morrow,
  For Death on earth brings pain and thrall:
Each heart must know its part of sorrow,
  But comfort waits alike for all.

One wretch alone no grace redeemeth,
  One groans all comfortless alone:
Woe, woe to him, who none esteemeth,
  Whose sullen heart is warm'd to none.

Children of God, whate'er betide you,
  In life or death like brothers still,
Grieve not for good to-day denied you;
  Wait the good hour, for come it will.

Long is the night to him that waketh,
  Short night is his whose sleep is sound:
God grant us joy when morning breaketh,
  God shield our rest while night goes round!

FROM LUIS DE LEON.

(Printed in the *Lyra Mystica*, edited by the Rev. Orby Shipley.)

HYMN TO CHRIST CRUCIFIED.

THOU Spotless Lamb of God,
    Bathed in Thine own dear Blood,
That flows to wash the world's deep guilt away,
    Who on the stubborn Tree
    Dost seem to call on me,
With Arms outstretch'd, to find the Grace I pray;
    Ere yet life's slow decay
    Makes pale the lustre bright
    Of that celestial Face,
    And Death's cold fingers trace
Their darkening shadows o'er those Orbs of light,
    O let one glance be thrown
From Thy meek Eyes on me, to mark me for Thine
        Own!

    Now when Thy Love profound
    Hath reach'd its utmost bound,

Nor mortal veil such Might may more confine;
    While on the painful Rood,
    With sharpest anguish bow'd,
Thy thorn-crown'd Head Thou dost to earth incline,
    With Mercy's glance Divine
    Thy Mother's gaze to meet;
    And Thy majestic Prayer
    E'en rebel souls would spare,
Sent upward to Thy Father's Glory-seat;
    O let Thy Pardon free
Prevail for sins like mine. Now, Lord, remember me!

    Now, while Thy suffering Hands
    Thy bounteous Grace expands,
As though in dying still outstretch'd to give;
    And, as in balance weigh'd,
    The full account is paid,
Whereby poor slaves redeem'd from bondage live;
    Thy captive, Lord, receive;
    While every vital pore,
    With flowing Mercy rife,
    Bursts out, and parting life
Drains from Thy heart Love's ne'er exhausted store;
    Fain would I first be there,
My loss, All-righteous Saviour, earliest to repair.

    Thy Bedesman, Lord, behold,
    In thraldom dark and cold

Long laid, entangled long in Error's chain :
    Yet Hope, o'ermastering Fear,
    Still prompts, that Thou wilt hear,
My Advocate will not my prayer disdain :
    Since Mercy's highest strain
    Decrees, that pardon free
    E'en there should most abound
    Where deepest guilt is found ;
And when the darkest stain is cleansed by Thee,
    Thy Blood with richest cost
Is lavish'd, and Thy Godlike love rejoiceth most.

    What though with guilty load
    My drooping neck is bow'd
And my sad spirit faints with toil and care,
    Because my rebel pride
    Cast Thy mild Yoke aside,
Doom'd, justly doom'd, a tyrant's bonds to bear :
    What though I might despair
    With weary steps and slow
    To reach Thee, Thou art nigh,
    And never more wilt fly ;
Those royal Feet transfix'd Thy purpose show ;
    Fix'd on the firm-set Tree
In patient grief they tell how Mercy waits for me.

    I know it, O my God :
    As in a quiet road

My good desires may here at anchor ride;
    That Heart, in open sign
    Of pitying Love Divine,
Seen through the lattice of Thy wounded Side,
    Hath all my need supplied:
    That to the dying Thief
    Gave comfort; one brief word
    He spake, and he was heard:
E'en as a glad surprise the pray'd relief
    The Answer gave; the night
Of darkness left his soul in dawn of Life and Light.

    I come in happy hour
    To feel Thy Grace's power,
Now, when with charter new, embracing all,
    Thy Gifts Thou dost prepare
    For all who seek to share:
Now, when to Thy sad Mother, bow'd in thrall,
    Thy sovereign Voice doth call,
    And bids her find a Son,
    Bids John a Mother find,
    The thief of contrite mind
To look for promised joy—shall I alone
    Still pine for Grace denied?
No, Lord! each empty soul with Thee is satisfied.

    Behold me, Lord, a son
    In error's path undone,

My portion lost, did Justice speak my doom:
    But Thy good word hath said
    That Mercy's mildest aid
Turns, stays, and guides repentant wanderers home.
    I come, Dear Lord, I come
    To kiss Thy sainted Feet,
    As on a rack, outspread
    On Thy hard dying bed;
For here my sorrowing voice Thy Grace shall meet,
    And Grace to Sons forgiven
Here speaks—O lost and found, thy portion rests in
    Heaven.

    For token of that Grace
    To all who seek Thy Face,
E'en now Thy Head in death Thou dost incline:
    I know that I have won
    Of Thee that priceless Boon,
The earnest of my hope, in that dear Sign.
    O Majesty Divine,
    O Love of Truth so pure,
    Thy Bounty to bequeath,
    That the Testator's death
Must pass to make the gift of Blessing sure!
    O mercy great and high,
That to confirm the bond e'en Mercy's Lord must
    die!

My Song, we here must stay :
Such theme to honour best
Not words, but flowing tears, should speak the rest :
Sad silent musings chase loud songs away :
Our notes we cannot keep,
When Earth is hush'd, and Sun and Heaven in darkness weep !

FROM GONGORA.

CAROL ON THE FESTIVAL OF THE PRESENTATION.

OH haste thee, shepherd, run and fly like silent bird on wing:
Oh see what hands the snow-white dove, the thankful offering, bring:
And see what aged man this day the gift of joy receives,
The gift a Maiden Mother bears, and as a Mother gives.

Oh let us mount with silent foot the solemn Temple-stair;
The Dove with olive-bough of Peace, the long-desired, is there;
The Hope fulfill'd of Simeon old, that comforts all his pain;
And, like the phœnix born anew, he breathes and lives again.

The fairest window of the fane, whereon the daystar bright
Was wont its eastern rays to pour, now beams with holier light:
A heavenly Sun hath dawn'd within, more bright than eastern sky:
The radiance glows on Simeon's breast, and fires his age-worn eye.

Oh hear! between the dove's soft moans a voice is heard more strong;
The grey old swan is pouring forth his last rejoicing song:
"Now, Lord, e'en now I part in peace; life hath no further store;
Mine eyes have Thy Salvation seen,—Thine, Lord, but ours much more."

Oh haste thee, shepherd, run and fly like silent bird on wing:
And see what hands the snow-white dove, the thankful offering, bring:
And how that old, old man in joy the gift of joy receives,
The gift a Maiden Mother bears, and as a Mother gives.

FROM CALDERON.

"HEAV'N'S GIFTS OF PARDONING LOVE."

Heav'n's gifts of pardoning Love
The sands upon the shore outnumber not,
Nor stars of night serene, the sparks of fire,
The golden motes of light, nor viewless wings
That bear the subtle chariot of the wind.
This I believe; and for this faith would give
Not one life only, but a thousand lives,
Were life and death now trembling in the scale.

THE POWER OF THOUGHT.

I AM the primal beryl-stone,
    That doth of Fortune's turns forewarn,
Of hue more changeful than the Moon,
    More glancing than the darts of Morn.

A homeless wanderer from my birth,
    I rove without commandment free
Through air and water, heaven and earth,
    And know not where my rest shall be.

Alike in grief and mounting joy
    The nimble spirits feel me near;
Mine the young dream of girl or boy,
    And man's or woman's hope and fear.

I am in kings—the uneasy watch,
    That o'er their realm and state they keep:
And rack their favourites to despatch
    The cares that break their masters' sleep.

I rule when great men's dooms are just:
    I wake remorse for sinner's crime;
I prompt the poor aspirant's trust,
    And wary placeman's trick of time.

Fair lady's boast of beauty bright,
    Brave gallant's vaunt of favour vain,
And daring-do in hardy knight,
    And gamester's stake of loss and gain,

Are mine : the miser's golden hoard
    I count, and bid the spendthrift groan;
I strike the glad heart's merriest chord
    And tune dejected sorrow's moan.

Yes, here and there, and everywhere
    I roam, unbound to place or plan;
Each guise assume, and then forswear;—
    The restless Thought of changeful man.

Yet call me not a thing of nought:
    This varied mood, this shifting strife,
Bears witness to the life of Thought;
    For where Thought comes not, what is Life?

The rainbow's hues my vest adorn;
    Such weeds doth mirthful Frenzy wear;
Yet deem me not of wit forlorn;
    Calm Reason did the garb prepare.

For who among the madmen gay
    More meetly should go forth attired,
Than he who dared to do or say
    Whate'er his motley Thought inspired?

All, all are mad; but all the praise
  Of sober sadness fain would win,
And but in hour unguarded raise
  The veil that hides the mood within.

Mine is that inner mood: whate'er
  Imperial Judgment's doom may be,
It cannot bind the shapes of air,
  With Thought still ranging, madly free.

Yet not in wildness bold and blind
  Without rebuke or check I stray:
The harp, whose chords obey the wind,
  Will more the Master's hand obey.

Though oft in Fancy's wayward hour
  Be heard her loud unmeasured tone,
Sweet chimes of more enduring power
  Ring out, when Thought and Truth are one

Then on my tower of watch I seek
  The Spirit of the mightier rhyme,
And Thought the Prophet guides to speak
  Of things unheard by Change and Time.

FROM AN UNKNOWN AUTHOR.

The following specimen of the Poetical Gloss, a favourite exercise of the Spanish Poets, is translated from a copy in the Translator's Folio MS. It is by an unknown Author; but the Poem itself appears to be well known in Spanish Literature.

DIALOGUE OF THE BODY AND SOUL.

"In the year 1500 a poet at Madrid composed the following octave; and just as he finished writing the last verse, he died a sudden death: but he had confessed himself the same day."—*MS. Note.*

How long the account to give of time prolong'd!
　The term how short! the call that none can stay!
The judgment-throne with thousand terrors throng'd,
　At which e'en Saints may tremble with dismay!
Duty undone! Heaven's holiest precepts wrong'd!
　The Judge how just, that will all wrongs repay!
Dread moment, when from God no force shall sever,
Or in the abyss of woe we pine for ever!

GLOSS ON THE ABOVE.

I.

What ails thee, my sad soul? 'Tis time to part.
   To part? from whom? From thee, whose load I
      bear.
When must thou go? To-day. Is there no art
   That can detain thee? None! no art, or prayer.
And hast thou joy, or sorrow? Both have part;
   Joy, to be free from earth-born fear and care:
Sorrow, to think of Heaven's just precepts wrong'd,
And of the long account of time prolong'd.

II.

The long account? of what? Of my sad sins.
   Of time prolong'd? What time? My life's whole
      span.
What, when the account is render'd? Doom begins.
   Thy doom? High God's dear blessing or deep
      ban.
But what weighs now against thee? Those dark
      lines
   Recording how with thee in guilt I ran.
Hast thou no hope? I hope; yet doubts dismay:
The term so short,—the call that none can stay!

III.

The term so short? of what?   Of life now fleeting.
   And what the call that none can stay?   Of death.
Is death so near?   So near, there's no retreating.
   Why thus?   Fate claims e'en now my forfeit breath.
But what is thy chief dread?   That thy poor cheating
   Led me enthrall'd to work my own sad scathe.
But what harm caused I?   Much: with thee I wrong'd
The judgment-throne with thousand terrors throng'd.

IV.

What judgment-throne?   The fearful throne of God.
   What terrors throng it?   First, the accusing sprite;
Then, man's ill conscience, and the avenging rod,
   That strikes on wretches banish'd from Heaven's light.
And what comes after judgment?   Driven and awed
   By vengeful furies still to pine in night,
The flock of lost ones to that realm shall stray,
At which e'en Saints may tremble with dismay.

V.

Why should Saints tremble?   For that Saints they are.
   If Saints they are, why fear?   Lest God chastise.
What cause?   That imperfection they too share.
   Yet Saints they are?   Saints, seeking Heaven's high prize.

But who should blame them? Their own jealous care.
   And who shall judge? Themselves; for they are wise.
But what ill find they? Much in life prolong'd;
Duty undone! Heaven's holiest precepts wrong'd!

VI.

Heaven's precepts wrong'd? how? By committed fault.
   Duty undone? when? In each fault's commission.
How doth God punish? When the soul hath sought
   His grace, and finds it not. Is that condition
So sad? So sad, all other woe is nought;
   For joy is none, save in that blest fruition.
And fear they this? They fear the impending day,
And that just Judge, that will all wrongs repay.

VII.

How is His justice shown? In speaking doom.
   Repaying whom? The guilty, doom'd to moan:
For Mercy then, long-slighted, finds no room.
   What most avails? Accepted labour done.
And what the accepted's portion? Not to come
   To wailing. What the lost one's? Still to groan
In anguish, lost the crown of good endeavour,
The moment, when from God no force shall sever.

VIII.

No force shall sever? how? No term of years
   Shall break those joys with relish ever new.
What things shall then have end? Deceits and fears.
   What good begin? Possession firm and true.
And bliss therewith? Bliss strange to mortal ears.
   What goes before? One moment, ere to view
Shall break that bliss, from which no force shall sever,
Or in the abyss of woe we pine for ever.

FROM VICENT GARCIA.

TO A VERY TALL LADY, MARRIED TO A LITTLE MAN.

Joanna, all our folks are glad
    To see you wed: but why, or how
Content thee with so small a lad,
    No bigger than a bird on bough?

They say, who see you side by side,
    Bridegroom so short, with bride so tall,
"How came that Sparrow, in his pride,
    To perch by that high belfry-wall?"

Or if you go for market-stuff,
    Where dealers balance weight and bale,
They say, "That lass might weigh enough,
    Without her make-weight in the scale."

At table-board, when flesh or fish
    Invite you, you appear, when seen,
Proportion'd like the great top-dish,
    And he, the little sauce-tureen.

The parson, ere his part began,
    Not knowing what he was to do,
Ask'd you, you know, "What little man
    Is this, who comes to church with you?"

For, seeing you, how grand you were,
    And him so very small a thing,
He took you for his Godmother,
    Who brought him to his christening.

FROM TOMAS DE YRIARTE.

A FABLE.

"The painful writer racks his brain
To please the vulgar herd, in vain.
What need of better prose or verse
For fools who prize and praise the worse?"
Thus spoke a Playwright, to excuse
The follies of his trashy Muse,
In a sly Poet's listening ear:
Now what the Poet answer'd, hear:
"An Ass, long patient of the pack,
Fed at his frugal owner's rack,
Grinding beneath his weary jaw
His daily portion of chopp'd straw,
Without complaint, though suffering long;
Till, adding insult to the wrong,
His master spoke: 'Take this, dull creature,
Since this contents your low-born nature.'
Poor Dapple, not quite unconcern'd,
Took heart, and answer meet return'd:
'I take it, since I must, hard man;
Digest it, as my stomach can;
But if for oats, which you deny me,
You think I have no relish, *try me.*'"

A FABLE.

It was a sturdy Warrener
    Came home at set of sun,
His pack of rabbits slung behind
    To show his work was done:
And hot and tired he seem'd to be,
But proud of his grand sport was he.

He met a neighbour: "Friend," he said,
    "My luck I needs must tell;
'Tis true the morning sun was hot,
    But I'm rewarded well.
See what a load I bear; 'tis more
Than ever mortal caught before.

"Without a boast I dare affirm
    I'll say and say again,
There's not a better warrener
    Than I am, in all Spain."
He look'd so grand and talk'd so loud,
'Twas very plain the man was proud.

He carried in his hand a box:
    Of cork the sides were made;
A ferret through the network'd door
    Poked out its snout and head.

For he had wonder'd much to hear
The talk of our vain warrener.

" My Master, by your leave," he said;
  " Two little words with you :
Pray, my dear sir, who caught that game?
  Which was it of us two?
Methinks in common equity
You might have said one word for me."

Perchance, dear Reader, you may think
  Our warrener would be
Corrected by this wise reproof:
  But was he? no, not he.
He braved it out; whate'er was done
The praise he counted for his own.

In short, he stood as much unmoved,
  As I have seen a knave
Who stole another's rhymes, and took
  The praise his hearers gave,
Without a word his debt to tell
To him who made him rhyme so well.

SONNET.

One morning by a wayside Cross there sate
   An Andalusian, somewhat droll and sly;
   When on an Andalusian horse came by
A Portuguese, in pride of place and state:
He look'd upon the native, and his hat
   He doff'd, as moved by well-bred courtesy:
   Like courtesy not wishing to deny,
Wearing a cap, the native took off that.
" My reverence, Zur, to you I did not make,"
   Said he of Portugal, unkindly proud,
" But to the Cross, which there uprear'd I see."
" Hush!" answer'd straight the other: " no mistake!
   To you I bow'd not, but your bit of blood,
A well-bred Andalusian, like to me."

FROM THE SPANISH.

See *Romancero General:—Agustin Duran.* Madrid, 1851.

THE CAPTIVE, A ROMANCE.

From a Castle's frowning turret thus a captive made his wail:
" 'Tis the joy of May returning, life and health in every gale.
Joyous sings the warbling linnet, answering to the nightingale.
'Tis the time when youthful lovers go to serve where love commands.
All but I, in darksome prison bound with misery's iron bands.
Scarce I know when morn's pale lustre through my narrow grating steals;
Scarce the change at evening twilight night's returning gloom reveals.
Late one little bird at dawning caroll'd, sweet his matin song;
But an archer shot my songster;—ill betide him for the wrong!

From my head the tangled elf-locks clustering fall
    below my knee,
And my beard so long and matted for a napkin
    serves for me.
My long nails are grown like talons, sharp as any
    scrivener's knife;
—If my King commands it, patience!—he may well
    command my life.
If the jailor wills it, traitor to my royal lord's command,
Patience yet;—so mean a traitor ne'er shall stain my
    knightly hand.
But alas! Could I but find me one of those poor
    mimic birds,
Taught in bowers of gentle ladies to repeat a teacher's
    words,
Were it thrush or merry linnet or the plaintive nightingale,
He should tell my gentle lady how to rid me of my
    bale:
"Leonora," he should tell her, "let your skilful hands
    prepare
For your captive knight a pasty of construction rich
    and rare:
Not with spotted trout or salmon fill the dainty dish
    within,
But with good steel-file and pick-lock, that deliverance
    he may win;

With a file to file his fetters, and a pick-lock for the
  door."
The good King was listening near him: "Prisoner,
  plan those tricks no more:
Let thy lady spare her pasty: open stands the
  prison-door."

A slightly different form of this ballad is given by Lockhart, under the title of *The Captive Knight and the Blackbird.*

DEATH OF DURANDARTE.

By the track where Durandarte late was borne with bleeding wound,
Sad and slow did Montesinos thread the mountain pass profound.
'Twas the hour when scarce the dawning lights the wakeful pilgrim's way,
When the steeple-clocks of Paris rang the chime of rising day.
Weary came the knight from battle; batter'd was the mail he wore;
In his strong right hand a fragment of his shiver'd lance he bore:
Shiver'd, yet a soldier's trophy; for the pointed steel was lost
In the corpse of Abenzaydi, bravest of the Moorish host.
This the knight of France bore onward, for it served him at his need
For a staff to wake the spirit of his way-worn battle steed.
Wearily he track'd the mountain, sadly gazing where the pass
By the day-beam brighter gleaming show'd the blood-empurpled grass.

Sadly beat the hero's bosom: terrors for himself unknown,
Stole upon his heart, revolving what brave friend was here o'erthrown:
Till amidst his doubt and sadness, from a beech-tree's spreading shade
Came a voice that seem'd to call him where a wounded knight was laid.
'Twas a voice whose tones of anguish pierced the champion's heart with woe:
Long he gazed upon the dying ere he could his features know.
Long he gazed, for his barr'd ventail dimness o'er his sight had spread,
Till he lighted from his charger, and disarm'd his helmed head.
Then he knew his own brave cousin, whom he loved in life most dear:
Close he drew, and bending o'er him strove his dying words to hear.
'Twas a sight the brave might pity, where those noble knights in woe
Show'd such heart-o'ermastering sorrow as the brave alone can know.
To th' unwounded spake the wounded, while th' unwounded clasp'd him round,
Weeping loud with such strong anguish that all words in tears were drown'd:

Till at length in dying accents thus his last commands
    he gave:
"Cousin dear, good Montesinos, low in death are
    laid the brave.
Low is laid the noble Roland;—woe is me for Alda
    fair!
Captive is the stout Guarinos, first in arms to do and
    dare.
Wounded sore, I feel within me near my heart death's
    cold arrest;
One poor boon I crave, one only, ere my spirit leave
    my breast.
From this corpse, now scarcely heaving, when the
    tenant soul shall part,
With this little poniard opening my left side, take out
    my heart.
And to fair Belerma bear it, lovely lady of my
    vow;
Tell her how I loved her living, how in death I love
    her now.
For that heart which dead I send her ne'er in life its
    faith belied.
All my good broad lands and lordships in the realm
    of France so wide,
Hers they are, to her I give them; 'tis the law for
    vassals true
To account their goods and chattels ever their dear
    sovereign's due."

Scarce his words the knight had ended, when his
    spirit seem'd to part :
Love was strong, but death had broken Durandarte's
    gallant heart.

DON RAMIRO.

There is strife in Aragon,—from Tolosa to Navarre;
All the nobles are at strife, foul debate and threats of war:
For their king is dead and gone; new pretenders seek to reign;
But the loyal keep their faith, firm and pure from treason's stain.
He that rules in Aragon must with right the throne obtain;
He must be of kingly blood;—meaner suitors ask in vain.
Don Ramiro's was the right, though a cloister'd monk was he;
Holy man he was as ever sprang from kingly pedigree;
King Alfonso's royal brother:—he their king of right must be.
So they take him from his cloister, though it pleased him not at all,
And proclaim him king and sov'reign, high in Huesca's royal hall.
Prosperous man was he in battle, happy in each venturous road;
Loved he was by all his vassals, gifts and graces he bestow'd.
But when first he fought the Paynim, 'twas a marvel then to see

How his gallant knights prepared him for his deeds
    of chivalry.
First they arm'd him with a breastplate strong to
    keep his heart's blood warm ;
Mounted him on warlike charger, with a shield on
    his left arm :
And his right hand bore his falchion bare and flashing
    in the sun :
But he needed further counsel ere th' array was duly
    done :
"Take the reins, dread lord," they said ; "take them
    in that selfsame hand
Where the shield is clasp'd ; then riding strike the
    Moor with trenchant brand."
Don Ramiro, sore perplex'd, answer'd thus his
    knights again :
"With the hand that holds the buckler I can never
    grasp the rein :
Put the bridle in my teeth ; then I may with comfort go."
As the king had so commanded, 'twas agreed it
    should be so.
Thus he enter'd into battle ; many a recreant Moor
    he slew :
Bravely many a time he bore him, and his realm with
    conquest grew.
Till at length he left his throne, and, as he had first begun.
Sought again his peaceful cloister till his sands of life
    were run.

AN ANDALUSIAN EPITAPH ON AN INFANT.

WHITE roses crown her brow :—mourn not thy loss,
  Sad mother!—not with palm from conflict done,
  But pure and fair her innocent soul is gone,
And on her breast sweet flowers entwine her cross.

Her death was as the dreams of infants are :
  Angels of light on her new waking smiled :
  One only want she knows, that happy child,
One only want in heaven,—till thou art there !

FROM MODERN SPANISH POETS.

DON LLUIS ROCA. JOCHS FLORALS DE BARCELONA, 1860.

THE DYING GIRL TO HER MOTHER.

I do not repine, sweet mother,
    I do not repine;
'Tis my lot, and I am ready,
    Since the lot is mine.

Nay, this day I feel me happy,
    Happy to be gone,
Since the Blessed Bridegroom seeks me,—
    He, the Eternal One.

Joy hath fill'd me at His coming,
    Joy to hear His call;
'Tis the trusting soul's last comfort,
    Comfort chief of all.

Hark, it sounds,—the voice that spake it,—
    Still the sound I hear;
From henceforth I fear no evil,
    Never more will fear.

One poor boon I crave, dear mother,
   One poor boon alone,
That thou make no moan at parting,
   Oh no, make no moan.

We are Christians, maid or mother,
   Taught the Christian skill
To resign us, when God willeth,
   Since it is His will.

Think, the soul in dying dies not,
   If in grace it dies;
In its aims to God transported,
   Far as aims can rise.

Think, though we, brief mortal flowers
   Live, like flowers, a day;
Flowers, whose sweetness mounts to heaven,
   Pass not all away.

There, oh there, shall I be waiting,
   Waiting there at home,
Till thou too shalt come, dear mother,—
   Thou in turn shalt come.

Where my place of rest is given,
   Thou that rest shalt share;
There we two shall dwell for ever,—
   Dwell in union there.

Dry thy tears, my own sweet mother,
    Dry thy tears for me;
More a day of joy than mourning
    Happy death should be.

Happy be the death-bell tolling,
    Happy signal-call!
Happy be the soul's last comfort,—
    Comfort chief of all!

DON ANTONIO DE TRUEBA: LIBRO DE LOS CANTARES.—LEIPZIG, 1860.

DIVIDED HEARTS

I.

Ramona.

"Come, dress me, dear Mary: come twine me with care
Each ringlet and braid of my bonny brown hair;
This day of all days on my looks I set store,
For a crisis is coming which ne'er came before."
"My young lady, you look like a newly blown rose,
When the first rays of morning the blossom unclose;
But be kind to my five wits, which run in a maze
To imagine why this is the day of all days."
"Because this fine day my fine bachelors three
Have each in their turn craved a hearing of me.
There is Geoffrey, and Lucas, and Robert the Grand,—
I would fain please them all, but can give but one hand.
"O charming! a marriage is then in the wind;
But to which of the pleaders will judgment be kind!"
"Fy, fy, without hearing no judge can decide;
The culprit's confessions the verdict must guide."

"Yes; but don't play the prude; take men as they are.
Let your words be well weigh'd : let your treaty be fair.
Play your game with decision; strike bravely your ball,
These are days when 'tis well to find husbands at all."
"But I bargain for one thing." "Oh, what may it be?"
"I bargain, that he, who makes contract with me
Should love me and me only; if not, let him go;
Without this condition my word will be No.
A heart undivided I ask and require,
I can never take half, when I give mine entire."

II.

GEOFFREY.

"Ramona, how dost thou?" "I'm well; how are you?"
"I'm badly; but still with your help I shall do."
"With my help?" "Yes." "But how?" "'Tis the
  simplest of things;
Be my wife, and I ask not the treasures of kings."
"Well, but first let the matter be well understood;
For the case needs a sober and serious mood.
I must tell you the truth; I'm a jealous poor thing."
"O Ramona, I'll never shoot bird on the wing,
Pigeon, partridge, or plover, white, black, brown, or
  grey,
If e'er from thy beauty my fancy shall stray."

"But, to come to the point, and to aid all debate,
Do you love any other?" "No more than I hate.
I am ready to swear in the world there is none
That I prize but yourself, and my dogs and my gun."
"O ho! so your dogs are your darlings, you say:
I shall wed, and find rivals in Fido and Tray.
Farewell, my dear Geoffrey; whate'er you endure,
With me for physician your case is past cure."
"Ramona, Ramona, you're mad." "If I be,
Put your hand on your mouth, for we ne'er shall
   agree.
A heart undivided I ask and desire;
Never offer me half, when I give mine entire."

III.

Lucas.

"Gentle maiden, may I with your leave now be
   heard?"
"Not more welcome the cuckoo when May hath
   appeared."
"O lovely as Dian whose orb is so bright
Cytherea with envy might swoon at the sight."
"Hold, hold! in the name of Paul, Peter, and John,
Let me hear you discourse like a Christian man's son,
Not in old Pagan nonsense." "Well then, let me
   speak

In plain terms, if you like not my fine heathen
    Greek.
Sweet lily, sweet rose, sweet carnation, so fine
With all hues of fresh beauty, with face so divine,
That no garden of earth with such bloom may
    compare."
" By this talk you are making my face a *parterre*."
" Nay, rather an Eden, for which my pure sigh
Love wafts to a Paradise over the sky.
Alas! if I gain it not, then I'm prepared . . . ."
" Heaven help us!" . . . " to die like a resolute bard.
I walk with two pistols, primed, loaded with ball,
One in each of my pockets; whate'er may befall,
The world shall not say 'twas a bully's vain boast."
" Then to keep you in life, lest your aim should be
    cross'd,
Let me ask what you seek?" " Your white hand is
    my aim."
" I'm free to bestow it without hurt or maim.
But first I must question, Pray tell me in truth,
Are you bound to none other by bond or by
    oath?"
" No bond or engagement my heart ever knew;
I have sported with none save the Muses and you."
" But your love to the Muses, I guess, is full-grown?"
" Both by night and by day I adore them, I own."
" Oh, for pity forgive me, the part is not mine
To contend in the field with competitors nine.

I should come off with scratches.   Dear friend of the
    lyre,
You've partition'd your heart, while I give mine entire."

IV.

" My young lady, Don Lucas in dudgeon is gone;
Whether north to the Shetlands, or south to Ceylon.
He will emigrate somewhere in wrath and despair;
But the Muses will help him his sorrows to bear.
He will not blow his brains out; the case were too
    hard
Should a little coquette be the death of a bard."
" Say no more; here comes Robert the Grand." " My
    young lady,
Though this swain be a clown, yet his tenants at pay-
    day
Bring him many doubloons; throw your glove in his
    way;
If he takes up the challenge, your heart may be gay."

Robert.

" Your slave, fair Ramona, awaits your command."
" What a delicate speech from tall Robert the Grand!"
" So blooming your charms and so trim your attire,
Pretty creature! your graces blind moles might admire."
" Sharp-eyed lynxes were better; but, flattery apart,
Let us come to our business;—unbosom your heart."

"Well then, I am rich; I have houses and land,
I have horses and coaches, and money in hand.
I have twenty fine girls even now in my view;
I might choose where I please, but I'd rather have you.
I have sported and fancied, been merry and gay;
But it seems after all but a contraband way.
In short I've concluded, I hope you'll agree;
Among all pretty monkeys, Ramona for me."
"Then Ramona, my friend, as the symptoms declare,
Will unkindly dismiss you, the willow to wear."
"The willow! to me do you say it, who swim
In an ocean of gold? what nonsensical whim
Has possess'd you? Poor soul! let your fancy be known."
"Only this; he who loves me must love me alone."
"O idle pretensions of ages that were!
None but frights and old women such claims would prefer.
My philosophy tells me, as life flies on wings,
To take all that I can of material things.
And each lad now-a-days, whose large heart is his own,
Parts it out in fair slices; each lass to have one."
"Gentle sir, if your heart you have parted so free,
Seek out maids less exacting: waste none upon me.
One heart undivided I ask and require,
Your slice will not serve, when I give mine entire."

MY MOTHER.

"Blessed is she that believed."—St. Luke i. 45.

I.

"O hush thee, my darling, till night turn to day,
Though night-winds may whistle, and night-hounds may bay:
For angels shall shield thee from harm and from dread,
With golden wings watching unseen round thy bed."

Thus sang my sweet Mother to lull me to rest,
When my life was unclouded, untroubled my breast;
Soft as dew on mine eyelids sweet slumbers held sway,
Till morn came in gladness, and night turn'd to day.

They said that the night-wind was shrill, as it play'd
Round the cot where my head in soft cradle was laid;
They said that the night-hounds were howling aloud,
As the moon in her wane met the wild racking cloud:

But all the night long not a sound did I hear,
Save the lullaby song falling sweet on my ear;

And my dream was of angels with bright wings outspread,
That fann'd my soft slumbers and watch'd round my bed.
Still, still from that night angels guarded my rest:
'Twas the creed of my Mother:—her spirit be blest.

II.

" My son, my heart's treasure, O hear me forewarn;
In life's path of roses beware of the thorn:
After storm the poor seaman finds joy in the calm:
After martyrdom past comes the crown and the palm."

Thus, with tears flowing fast as the soft April rain,
Flow'd my Mother's sweet words at our parting of pain,
When I left my dear valley:—oh, ne'er will depart
That hour from my memory, that home from my heart.

Alas! for the mountain's green slopes, and the glade,
Where my brothers and I through the walnut-grove play'd:
Alas! for the holt, whose cool alleys along
The far wood-notes re-echoed the voice of my song:
Alas! for the covert with chestnuts o'ergrown,
And the white cot beneath them, how dearly my own!

I have roam'd through the world like a pilgrim
    forlorn :
Short-lived were its roses, long-lasting the thorn :
The pang at my heart can no comfort assuage :
Lo, the brow of my manhood is wrinkled with age.

But if God gives me sorrows, His promise pours
    balm :
"After martyrdom past comes the crown and the
    palm."
Return, my sad soul, to thy haven of rest ;
'Twas the creed of my Mother :—her spirit be blest !

III.

"My son, if thy heart hear the call of sweet Love,
Forget not, its birthplace, its home, is above.
Woe worth to the proud, who weak woman would
    wrong,
Be the strength of the feeble, the arm of the strong."

'Twas my Mother's sweet counsel ; her soul in
    each line
Spoke of Love as immortal, its life as divine :
May her spirit the crown of the seraphim wear,
Who taught me pure vows which the seraphs might
    share !

Thenceforward in Love I that essence behold
Whose bond doth the world in its concord enfold,
The source of all tenderness chaste and benign;
To pay it on earth in glad service be mine!

And woman to me is a plant, whose frail form,
Exposed in the rude world must bend to the storm,
Save when a supporter to shield and to guide,
Frank, noble, true-hearted, is near at her side.

This faith gives me joys to the vulgar unknown,
Words tell not their sweetness, I feel them my own.
O, holy the creed, in such faith that could rest!
'Twas the creed of my Mother:—her spirit be blest!

IV.

Once more, in sweet lines her last counsel she
    gave:—
"My son, be not sad, when I go to the grave.
'Tis nought but vain dust to this earth we resign:
The soul lives undying: its source is divine."

Thus wrote my sweet Mother: faith quelling all
    fear,
When she knew that her time of departure was near:
She is dead; she is number'd with beings that were:
But my heart ever speaks and holds converse with her.

There are beings I loved: they have made their
    last moan;
And I walk in this rude world a pilgrim alone.
But I reck not; O ne'er shall my spirit misgive!
Still with them I hold converse: they love and they
    live.

Whene'er for their tombstones a garland I wreathe,
Or defend their dear names from Imposture's foul
    breath,
They pray, with bright joy on each passionless brow,
To the Father of spirits to prosper my vow.

O creed of the holy and humble of heart,
Ne'er, ne'er from my bosom thy power shall depart,
Making Friendship and Love in eternity rest:
'Twas the creed of my Mother:—her spirit be blest!

LOVE IMMORTAL.

I.

It was the hallow'd eve of rest,
   When, leaning from the balcony
We watch'd beyond the mountain-crest
   The glowing western sky.

A sadness of the twilight hour
   Was in my heart, and in her own;
For we were born to feel its power,
   To love, and love as one.

And chasten'd hope and pure desire
   Were breathing in each silent sigh,
While paler glow'd the parting fire
   That lit the western sky.

For in that hour, so sadly sweet
   When faintly gleams the sun's last ray,
And little birds half-hush'd repeat
   Their farewell to the day;

And o'er each fountain-side and stream
   The white mist hangs its vapoury shroud,
And the pale moon's victorious beam
   Darts through each wandering cloud;

And in the neighbouring village-tower
    The mellow chime is heard, that calls
To prayer at solemn evening hour
    Within the sacred walls;

My God! how sweet is then the thought
    Of love unblamed! but what the pain
To hearts, that answering love have sought
    Beguiled to hope in vain!

"Mary," I said, "I cannot rest:
    O tell me, must I sigh alone,
Nor find a chord within that breast
    Responsive to my own?"

The maiden downward turn'd her eyes
    In modest glance of maiden fear;
Then raised them to the darkening skies,
    For Heaven in thought was near:

And spoke as if her boding heart
    The darkening future could divine:
"There, where no change the bond can part,
    Shall meet thy love and mine."

II.

The love that happy children know,
    Increasing as their days increase;
The love with which bright angels glow,
    All purity and peace;

Such love was ours:—the year went round:
    O God! the glory all be Thine;
Thy gift that love, which knew no bound,
    Pure, innocent, divine.

Who calls this world a vale of tears,
    Hath never felt that higher strain,
That nobler mood, wherein appears
    Lost Paradise again.

But ah! it could not, might not, last:
    That sweetest maid, whose childhood free
Gay birds or butterflies had chased
    Through woods, o'er lawns, with me:

That maid, so loving and beloved,
    Whose troth-plight now to me was given,
Whose heart from mine had never roved,
    Was not for earth, but heaven.

She droop'd, as droops a short-lived flower,
    She breathed the weary parting moan,
And to its amaranthine bower
    That angel-soul had flown.

A spirit from a brighter sphere,
    Awhile she wander'd, like the dove,
But found no rest on billows here,
    And sought her ark above.

Yet think not that in grief for her
    I wept with hopeless tear and sigh:
Such love is not of things that were,
    It dies not when we die.

The undying soul in mortal heart
    Hath yearnings, like itself, divine:
She spake it: "Where no change can part,
    Shall meet thy love and mine."

III.

I MOURN'D her, early dead,—not so
    As men past hope, past comfort, mourn;
But with such natural tears as flow
    From all of women born.

I mourn'd with trembling heart, resign'd,
    With hope o'ermastering mortal fears,
For her, whose love my fate had twined
    For evermore with hers.

Faith dried my flowing tears; and now
    My sighs uplift my soul to heaven:
My childhood's joy, my manhood's vow,
    Thy bonds of death are riven!

Those eyes of love still gaze on me,
    That gentle voice is still my stay;
I hear its tones, when wearily
    I toil in life's rude way.

Along the mead, or thro' the wood,
    Where'er in memory sad I mourn,
That gentle voice to my sad mood
    Comes answering in return.

My God! how sweet, how sweet is Faith!
    Beneath the western balcony,
Whence first our vows for life or death
    Were heard and mark'd on high,

There grows a little summer-flower;
    Her hands had rear'd and train'd it there;
Which every day at plighted hour
    Her message seems to bear:

"Forget me not, my only love:"
    The message in each bloom is set:
I answering gaze on heaven above:
    "I never can forget."

For why? she is not dead, whose breast
    Was leaning from the balcony,
When on that hallow'd eve of rest
    We watch'd the western sky,

When, with soft blush, her maiden's heart
    Spoke to my heart at day's decline:
"There, where no change the bond can part,
    Shall meet thy love and mine."

SONG.

THE HERB-MAIDEN.

I SAW thee on thy early round,
    Where thou didst take thy way
To cull thy herbs in garden ground,
    At dawn of golden day.

I went to take a nearer view,—
    No further thought in mind,—
But when I left the ground, I knew
    I'd left my heart behind.

What I have lost, 'tis thou hast found,
    It rests with none but thee:
Young maiden of the garden-ground,
    Give back my heart to me.

SEÑOR BIENVENIDO Y CANO.

ELEGY

ON ARGUELLES, CALATRAVA, AND ALVAREZ Y
MENDIZABAL, MINISTERS OF SPAIN.

The late distinguished ministers, Agustin Arguelles, José Maria Calatrava, and Juan Alvarez y Mendizabal, have had their remains deposited with many tokens of public honour in the cemetery of St. Nicolas and St. Salvador at Madrid; and the Spanish Muses have followed them, certainly in a spirit which affords a pleasing contrast to the scurril rhymes in which Villamediana sang the downfall of the statesmen of Philip III.'s reign, and some imitators of Villamediana pursued in his retirement the fallen Olivares. The following lines appear to be worthy of notice, not only for their elegiac pathos, but because the style reminds us that there is now in Spain a little reviving regard to the school of Gongora.

True genius dies not,—no: o'er death's dark sea
    Lies the far land the God of life defends;
And, borne in strength to Him, the spirit free
    Fills time's long ages, and all space transcends.

What boots it, if too soon the parting breath
    Leave the frail shroud, and Nature prompts to moan?
From life's steep pilgrimage it gains in death
    The portal of a world to death unknown.

Vainly the slave of gold with toil and pain
    Would stay the hours that in his sand-glass haste;
Through marble halls sad echo sighs, 'Tis vain
    To seek the blooms of spring in winter's waste.

The marble tomb, where banners proudly wave,
    Fills not with earnest tears the gazer's eye,
Like one poor flower that strews the peasant's grave,
    Or lowly cross that warns how man should die.

For virtue's rich memorial is the seed
    Of truth divine its patient hand hath sown,
And kindly Genius is its own fair meed,
    Felt in all hearts, the world's wide wealth its own.

Arguelles, Calatrava, Alvarez,
    Your virtuous worth in trinal union
Lived poorly, when to princely dignities
    Ye might have soar'd, and golden store have won.

But see your grateful land, on this fair day,
    Hallowing your names, a granite record raise,
While tones more clear than old Amphion's lay
    Chaunt to the rising pile your deathless praise.

Blest tomb, that, founded in a people's love,
    To that just love a holier ardour gives!
Blest, that such vow a people's heart could move,
    More blest for that high praise that with it lives!

No more: for generous deeds of godlike men
    Live evermore, emblazon'd on that scroll,
Whereof immortal spirits hold the pen,
    The conscious tablets of the undying soul.

FROM THE MODERN GREEK.

See *Chants populaires de la Grèce Moderne.*—Fauriel, 1825.

"WHY ARE THE MOUNTAINS OVERCAST?"

Why are the mountains overcast? what dim and darkening shroud
Rolls round with war of icy wind that drives the racking cloud?
'Tis not the storm-cloud in its gloom, or wind with icy breath:
It is the Hunter on his road: the sweeping blast of Death.
The young he drives before his face; the old, too weak to go
He drags behind; pale infant-forms are on his saddle-bow.
With bended knee both young and old beseech him on his way:
"Good rider, draw thy rein one hour before our home to stay:
Before our village home the fount flows cool beneath the tree:
There let the old man slake his thirst, and let the young be free

One hour to ply their games of strength; the little
    child, one hour
To wander yet on earth's green lap, and pluck the
    budding flower.
List to the prayer, nor be the boon, one little boon,
    denied;
Let the sad mother clasp her child, the bridegroom
    bless his bride!"
"It may not be," the Pale One said; "the draught
    would wake again
The feeble old man's thirst of life, forgetful of its
    pain:
The young's desire would glow more fierce, resisting
    Heav'n's decree,
The wife and mother strive, more loth to yield their
    loves to me.
I stay not, till to other Powers my service I bequeath;
'Tis not of earth, though shown on earth, the Love
    that masters Death."

www.ingramcontent.com/pod-product-compliance
Lightning Source LLC
Chambersburg PA
CBHW031906220426
43663CB00006B/793